Physical Characteristics of the Portuguese Water Dog

(from the American Kennel Club breed standard)

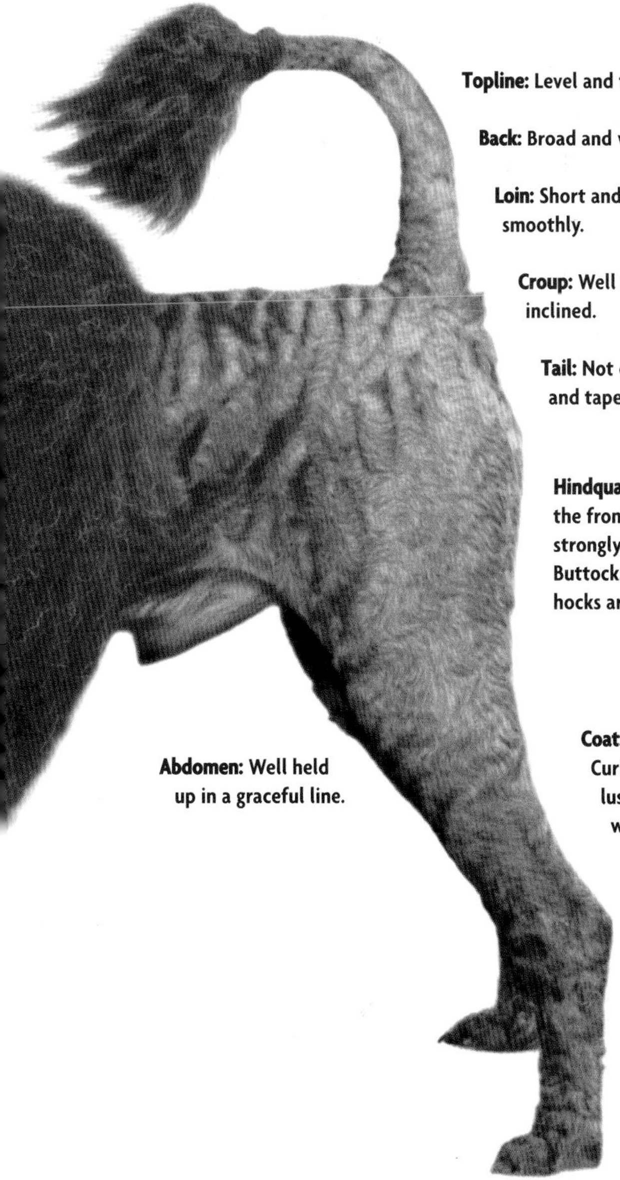

Topline: Level and firm.

Back: Broad and well muscled.

Loin: Short and meets the croup smoothly.

Croup: Well formed and only slightly inclined.

Tail: Not docked; thick at the base and tapering.

Hindquarters: Powerful; well balanced with the front assembly. Legs...straight and very strongly muscled in upper and lower thighs. Buttocks are well developed. Tendons and hocks are strong.

Abdomen: Well held up in a graceful line.

Coat: There are two varieties of coat: Curly—Compact, cylindrical curls, somewhat lusterless. The hair on the ears is sometimes wavy. Wavy—Falling gently in waves, not curls, and with a slight sheen.

Color: Black, white, and various tones of brown; also combinations of black or brown with white.

Portuguese Water Dog

By Paolo Correa

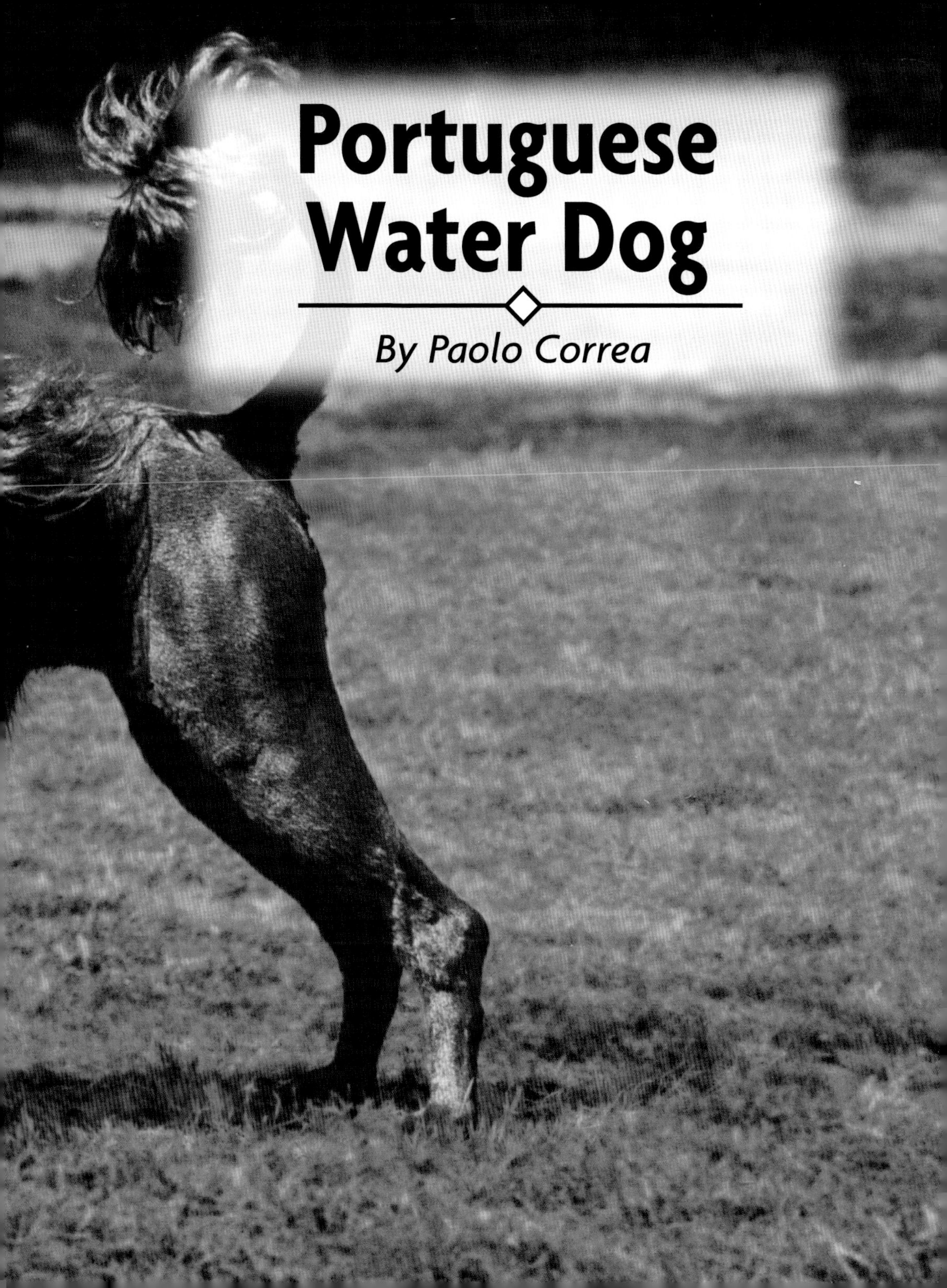

Contents

KENNEL CLUB BOOKS: **PORTUGUESE WATER DOG**
ISBN 13: 978-1-59378-286-3

40 Broad Street, Freehold, New Jersey, 07728 • USA
Cover Design Patented: US 6,435,559 B2 • Printed in South Korea

10 9 8 7 6 5 4 3 2

Photography by Carol Ann Johnson and Karen Taylor
with additional photographs by

Mary Bloom, Paulette Braun, T.J. Calhoun, Alan and Sandy Carey, Carolina Biological Supply, Isabelle Français, Bill Jonas, Dr. Dennis Kunkel, Tam C. Nguyen, Phototake, Jean Claude Revy and Alice van Kempen.

Illustrations by Patricia Peters.

The publisher wishes to thank all of the owners of the dogs featured in this book, including Jayne Johns and Valerie Marthaler.

A Portuguese Water Dog enjoys a romp in the surf. Whether working or playing, the breed has a natural love of water; it is one of the best water retrieving breeds in dogdom.

HISTORY OF THE

PORTUGUESE WATER DOG

When one thinks of a sporty, agile retriever, rarely does the Portuguese Water Dog come to mind. Yet this delightful Portuguese breed has many outstanding retriever qualities and is an excellent water dog. The breed's low profile is a result of its being overshadowed by some of the more recognized hunting dogs, such as the Labrador Retriever and Golden Retriever. However, the breed's low public profile has probably done it some good over the years. Since it is a relatively rare breed in many countries, it has continued to remain healthy and sound through responsible breeding programs and loyal devotees. Many of the popular breeds suffer from debilitating genetic conditions due to over-breeding practices, a fate that has not darkened the Portuguese Water Dog's portals.

Although the exact origin of the breed remains a mystery, there are a few theories that have withstood the test of time and have been accepted by most breed historians. The Portuguese Water Dog (or some dogs very closely resem-

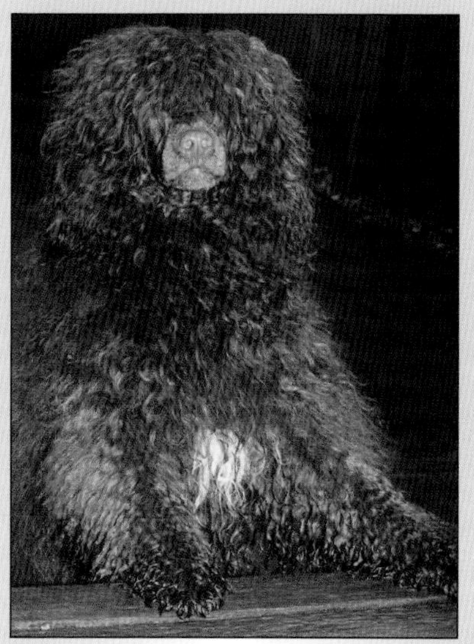

SWIMMING COUSINS

The Portuguese Water Dog is counted among the curly-coated water dogs who excel at retrieving. Among the related breeds are the Poodle and Barbet of France, the Irish Water Spaniel of Ireland, the Curly-Coated Retriever of the UK, the Perro de Agua (or Spanish Water Dog) of Spain, the Wetterhoun of the Netherlands and the American Water Spaniel of the US. All of these breeds share similar features, including a water-proof coat, exceptional swimming ability and uncanny intelligence.

bling it) definitely existed over 1,000 years ago. Some breed historians purport that the breed goes back to the eighth century, claiming that these dogs worked alongside fishermen on boats in what is now Portugal. Another theory claims that the confederation of German tribes known as the Goths brought these dogs back from the east. Consider also that the Berbers and their descendants the Moors brought the dogs to Europe via North Africa and Morocco, as one theory suggests. Some of these early dogs may have gone west to Germany and contributed to the gene pool of the Poodle. Certainly the Poodle and Portuguese Water Dog share many like features, not the least of which are their uncanny intelligence and their colorful curly coats.

As their name suggests, the Portuguese Water Dogs were—and continue to be—superb swimmers. In Portugal, the breed is known as the "Cão de Agua," which translates as "dog of the water." They were used on fishing boats and were sent to retrieve various items in what were sometimes adverse water conditions. These dogs retrieved damaged fishing nets and other fishing tackle. In addition, they also used their herding ability to gather the day's catch in nets. Occasionally they were even used to send messages between boats or to the shoreline. Despite their usefulness, the breed was eventually replaced by modern fishing techniques and equipment, which nearly caused their extinction.

Many believe that the Newfoundland and Chesapeake Bay Retriever may have influenced the later development of the Portuguese Water Dog, as these two breeds have many of the same physical characteristics as today's Portuguese Water Dog. Although there is no substantial evidence that these breeds were responsible for the Portuguese Water Dog's development, many breed historians believe there is a distinct connection.

INFLUENTIAL DOGS AND BREEDERS

Most of the modern influential Portuguese Water Dog breeders and their established stock can be traced back to the early 1930s. A dog named Leao is accepted as the founding sire of the modern Portuguese Water Dog. A gentleman by the name of Vasco Bensaude

CANIS LUPUS

"Grandma, what big teeth you have!" The gray wolf, a familiar figure in fairy tales and legends, has had its reputation tarnished and its population pummeled over the centuries. Yet it is the descendants of this much-feared creature to which we open our homes and hearts. Our beloved dog, *Canis domesticus*, derives directly from the gray wolf, a highly social canine that lives in elaborately structured packs. In the wild, the gray wolf can range from 60 to 175 pounds, standing between 25 and 40 inches in height.

The Chesapeake Bay Retriever may have influenced the development of the Portuguese Water Dog.

The Newfoundland has been cited in the ancestry of the Portuguese Water Dog. Three Newfoundland color varieties—Landseer, black and brown—are shown here.

from Portugal, who was a shipping tycoon, acquired Leao from an old fisherman. Leao sired seven litters and was admired for his extraordinary qualities. After watching Leao perform on the old man's fishing vessel, Bensaude immediately fell in love with the breed.

As his interest in the breed flourished, Bensaude developed his Algarbiorum Kennels. He would later become the secretary-general and founder of the Portuguese Water Dog Club. He would hold this position for several years and become a major influential figure in the breed.

As the years passed, Bensaude eventually resigned from his duties as club secretary-general and gradually relinquished his club responsibilities. Fearing the worst, he decided that he would need to go on an intensive search for someone who would be able to care for his dogs and kennel in case of his death. He would later meet up with Senhora Conchita Cintron de Costello Branco, a noted horsewoman, who came highly recommended from his veterinarian.

ORIGINS

Although a Portuguese breed, there is evidence of the PWD around the world at different points of its development. Some sources claimed that it can be traced back to 700 BC in the central Asiatic steppes and to the 8th century on the Iberian Peninsula. The breed made its way to British shores as working dogs on Spanish Armada ships in the late 1500s.

After meeting with Bensaude, Cintron accepted the responsibility and agreed to tend to Bensaude's kennel of dogs upon his death.

In 1967, Cintron's promise to the Bensaude family would become a reality. Bensaude's wife contacted Cintron and told her that her husband had passed away. True to her word, Cintron was now the proud owner of all of Bensaude's dogs. At first, Cintron knew very little about this unique breed, but that situation soon changed.

Cintron initially inherited 14 Portuguese Water Dogs from the Algarbiorum Kennel. Evidently, she was told that the dogs were difficult to breed and that many were, in fact, infertile. How very wrong these uninformed individuals were. This was soon revealed when Cintron found herself with 90 Portuguese Water Dogs to care for! A true nightmare for any breeder, despite his or her experience. Sra. Cintron's new kennel became known as Al-Gharb.

At the same time that Cintron acquired Bensaude's stock, the country of Portugal was experiencing severe financial difficulties. Cintron knew that she could never find appropriate homes for all of these dogs in her own country. Therefore she decided to appeal to dog lovers in the US and wrote letters to the Portuguese Embassy in Washington, DC. In her letters, she proudly described the magnificent qualities of these precious water dogs. Apparently, Cintron must have been very convincing and persuasive in her writing.

In July 1968, Deyanne and Herbert Miller from New Canaan, Connecticut acquired a breeding pair from Cintron. This would later become the start of the Portuguese Water Dog in the US. However, before discussing the breed's development in America, I must acknowledge a few of Portugal's outstanding Portuguese Water Dog

A WATER-LOVER BY ANY NAME

Because of its superb qualities as a water dog, the Portuguese Water Dog had several nicknames. It was known as the "Portuguese Fishing Dog", "Diving Dog" and "Sea Dog." Today, the breed continues to hold on to its exceptional water skills. It's used as an efficient hunter on both land and sea and frequently participates in sanctioned events that test the breed's water skills in recognized water-related competitions.

MODERN ADVANCEMENTS
Developments in radar methods and the use of radio and advanced equipment nearly caused the extinction of the Portuguese Water Dog. This highly intelligent working dog was also replaced by other contemporary fishing methods, which drastically reduced its popularity.

breeders. Dr. Cabral began his own family of dogs called the Alvalade line based on Silve's dogs. Carla Molinari inherited these dogs in her Vale Negro Kennels. Ana Victoria Ruivo, a resident of Faro, was a successful breeder for nearly 40 years. Ruivo was a major influence in establishing the breed's type, soundness and well-being in its native land.

THE PORTUGUESE WATER DOG IN AMERICA

The introduction of the Portuguese Water Dog to American soil was a slow process. Like most other rare breeds that are first introduced to a particular area, it took some time for the breed to gain the respect it rightfully deserved. In 1968 Deyanne and Herbert Miller imported a bitch named Chenze, who was the first Portuguese bitch import to arrive in the US. Chenze established herself as a producer of many offspring and lived to the impressive age of 15.

Despite Chenze's influence, many of her first offspring had some serious health problems. This made it quite difficult to find homes for her puppies and other Portuguese Water Dog litters that followed. Despite the breed's many fine qualities, many people were unwilling to take a chance with an unfamiliar breed.

During the 1960s, when many countries, including the US, were still recovering from financial difficulties from past wars, it was hard enough to find homes for dogs of breeds that had been in the country for decades. Therefore it was nearly impossible for a rare breed that had just recently arrived to establish a stronghold and substantial following. Fortunately, there was a handful of dedicated Portuguese Water Dog fanciers that was determined to keep the breed alive and well. These individuals were committed to do their best to produce healthier and sturdier dogs. This adamant group would go on to form the first club for the breed. In 1972, the Portuguese Water Dog Club of America was established. Its first president would be Herbert H. Miller, Jr.

The late Helen Roosevelt was one of the first Portuguese Water Dog owners, acquiring her first dogs in 1971. Many dogs purchased during this time period were from the Portuguese Al Gharb bloodline of Sra. Cintron. This particular line would be the last to land on American soil because of the Portuguese Revolution.

Dedicated Portuguese Water Dog aficionados loved the breed so much that they helped to overcome the obstacles that the breed faced in its early days in the US to produce sound, healthy and multi-talented dogs.

Ancora do Al Gharb arrived in the US in November 1969 and was the sire of 11 American litters. Breed interest continued to grow during the 1970s when there was a significant increase in the popularity of the Portuguese Water Dog. The Albergaria, Asaumbufa and Condinho Kennels were the dominant forces in the breed at this time.

As the 1980s rolled around, individuals like Beverly Jorgensen (longtime American breeder and fancier) were producing dogs that were fit, sound and multipurpose. In 1981, the American Kennel Club (AKC) accepted the breed in the Miscellaneous Class. The Portuguese Water Dog was accepted for registration in the AKC stud book in August 1983 and, by January 1984, the breed was eligible to compete in the AKC's Working Group. Ch. Charlie de Alvalade, "Charlie," became the first Portuguese Water Dog to become an American champion. Charlie had many admirers and was recognized for his excellent type and form.

It's impossible to list all of them, but some other noteworthy dogs that were responsible for the breed's development included: Ch. Farmion Geo, UD; Ch. Timbermist Lancar Flor de Mar, and Am. Can. Ch. Jewell De Aguas Windward Lad, CDX, Can. CD, WWD,

Those who have gotten to know the Portuguese Water Dog and discovered all of its wonderful attributes are hooked!

TT, CGC, PT. To go along with these illustrious dogs were the breeders, handlers and owners who were responsible for their great accomplishments. MaryAnne Murray (Brinmar Kennel) was the first owner-handler to put a conformation championship on a Portuguese Water Dog in the US. Cathy Kalb (Camerell Kennel) made her mark on the breed by excelling in the performance arena. Many of her dogs excelled in both obedience and agility. One of her most famous dogs was Call Me Cooper, CDX, AWD, AAD, ROM. Cooper was the first dog of any breed to obtain the Agility Dog title.

The list continues with Jane Harding (Cutwater Kennel), who produced over 40 conformation champions. Steven Dostie (Downeast Kennel), William J. Trainor (Farmion Kennel), Karen and Bob Arends (Seabreeze Kennel) and Robin Zaremba (Windward Kennel) are just some of the other top-notch Portuguese Water Dog powerhouses who made their mark on the breed. Many of them continue to do so, even to the present day.

THE PORTUGUESE WATER DOG IN THE UK

Upon its arrival, the Portuguese Water Dog was even less popular in England than in its early days in the US. The breed first arrived in the UK in the 1950s, and most if not all of these original imports eventually died out. It wasn't until 1979 and 1980 that the breed was imported once again. Trish Gilpin and Paddy Holbrook O'Hara can be credited with the breed's resurrection in the UK.

Gilpin would be responsible for importing a pair of dogs that would later start the Glenwhin line. O'Hara imported two dogs by the names of Eveil and Panta de Alvalade, which were evidently given to a woman named Miss Pat Jones, who would later start the Cartmel line. In 1984, Cartmel the Fisherman would be the first of the breed to be exhibited at Crufts in Any Variety (AV). It wasn't until 1989 that the PWD had the first class of its own at the National Working Breeds Championship Show. By 1991, the Portuguese Water Dog had its own class at Crufts.

During the 1990s, the breed made a slow but upward spiral in popularity in the UK. A handful of British kennels have come into their own in recent years and have begun producing dogs that are of improved quality. Ruth and David Bussell (Brigantia Kennel), Cheryl Ducket (Coparit Kennel), Nigel Barrow (Elmley Kennel), Jayne Johns (Gemsons Kennel), Trish Gilpin (Glenwhin), Carol Queen (Grandways), Rachael Reddin (Rarjo), Sue Tweedie (Rysalka) and Patricia Jones (Cartmel) are some of the most respected and influential.

CHARACTERISTICS OF THE PORTUGUESE WATER DOG

IS THE PORTUGUESE WATER DOG RIGHT FOR YOU?

If you've been thinking about acquiring a Portuguese Water Dog, odds are you've probably started the research that's necessary before purchasing any breed of dog. You are prepared to commit yourself to dog ownership, and your interest in the PWD has led you to learn all you can about the breed. The Portuguese Water Dog's dedicated group of breeders and fanciers have worked hard to maintain the breed's stability. Breeders are very selective with their owners and do their very best to place dogs where they are most likely to receive the love and care they rightfully deserve.

The Portuguese Water Dog is extremely bright and active. Its uncanny intelligence can be very challenging to new owner(s). Portuguese Water Dog puppies can be very demanding. They require constant attention and cherish family interaction right through adulthood. They can be sensitive and should always be trained with positive reinforcement. If you choose a young puppy, expect him to chew anything that is easily accessible. The young Portuguese Water Dog has even been known to eat plants and other vegetation right down to the roots! They should be heavily supervised at all times and safely crated if left for extended periods of time.

The Portuguese Water Dog comes in two different coat types: wavy and curly; both types are equally acceptable. They have a robust stature and webbed toes, with a well-balanced and muscled physique. They are tremendous swimmers and have unique diving skills; these are rugged dogs that love to work outdoors. The

LIVING UP TO ITS NAME

As its name suggests, the Portuguese Water Dog is an excellent swimmer and diver. They have been known to leap great distances into the water and submerge themselves several feet deep into the water. When the breed was first introduced hundreds of years ago, they were frequently called upon to dive off fishing vessels to retrieve broken fishing gear and to herd schools of fish into nets.

breed's athleticism and intelligence have allowed it to excel in agility, flyball, obedience and even tracking. They are quick learners and eager to please their owners. At the same time, they can be extremely sensitive and their feelings are easily hurt.

The Portuguese Water Dog has sometimes been described as the "clown" of the water dog family. They seem to have sudden bursts of energy that come out of nowhere. Frequently, they can be found sitting calm and motionless. Then, only minutes later, they will be running around from room to room in an excited way. If you are looking for a calm, docile dog, the Portuguese Water Dog may not be the right one for you. They have a unique sense of humor that doesn't always sit well with some individuals. Daily exercise, and plenty of it, is an absolute necessity for the breed. A PWD is best suited to the active owner who enjoys long walks to an open field or park, or frequent visits to the beach or lake. The breed's excellent retrieving abilities make them good flying-disc dogs and perfect companions for simple fetching games.

Even though they are phenomenally successful as water dogs, Portuguese Water Dogs are just as valuable as family companions.

The Portuguese Water Dog is a quick learner. This is the reason why the breed has done very well in all types of performance and

WINNERS IN WATER

The PWDCA (Portuguese Water Dog Club of America) sanctions water trials that simulate many ancient functions of the breed. The club has underwater and fish net retrievals, message delivery (from one boat to another) and a measured distance swim. The Portuguese Water Dog enjoys these competitive water events, and these activities keep the dog in maximum shape and condition.

The Portuguese Water Dog is an extremely agile flying-disc dog. (ABOVE) He eagerly awaits the throw and then (BELOW) brings it back for a repeat performance.

sporting activities. They love to please their owners and will go to extremes to do so. They are energetic, affectionate and trustworthy, and they thrive on human attention. They bond very easily. Despite the breed's loyalty to its owners and immediate family, it can be reserved with strangers. In fact, PWDs make good watchdogs and will bark to alert you of possible danger when confronted with a stranger or the arrival of an unfamiliar car or person. The breed's bravery and independence are easily recognizable. The breed does very well with children and other animals. The Portuguese Water Dog's high energy will keep both the dog and your child busy for hours while they enjoy each other's company in play. Of course, any dogs and young children should always be supervised.

If you are looking for a dog that requires minimal grooming, you may want to look elsewhere. The Portuguese Water Dog requires consistent grooming that includes a firm brushing at least three times a week to remove mats and shed hair, which often becomes caught in the long coat. Although they do shed, they shed less than one might think for a heavily coated breed. In dog show competition, the breed is exhibited in one of two clips: the "lion" and the "retriever." With the lion clip, the hindquarters as well as the muzzle are clipped short. The end of the tail is left long and

HEIGHT AND WEIGHT

The male Portuguese Water Dog stands 20 to 23 inches and is usually between 42 to 60 pounds. The female version of the breed is smaller. She stands 17 to 21 inches high and is 35 to 50 pounds.

the coat on the head, neck, forequarters and chest is left long to resemble the lion's mane. The retriever clip is the choice of many pet owners; this is also acceptable for showing. If you decide to go with the retriever clip, the entire coat is scissored or clipped to a length of 1 inch, except the end of the tail, which is left long. If you are a new Portuguese Water Dog owner, it's probably best to contact your breeder or an experienced groomer before attempting to clip the dog yourself.

In the field, the breed can be taught to flush out upland game and water fowl. They are excellent retrievers with soft mouths. They even have a distinctive innate herding ability. Whether it's in the field or in the home, Portuguese Water Dogs make wonderful companions. They are truly "people dogs" and require the utmost respect and loyalty. If you're willing to give these dogs the attention and love they require, you will certainly receive that same respect back and learn the meaning of true friendship.

HEALTH CONCERNS

The Portuguese Water Dog is a healthy breed of dog. It's not uncommon for them to live well over 12 years of age. They are a strong breed and resistant to many of the common ailments that frequently affect some of their canine cousins. Before acquiring a new puppy, it's essential that he has a clean bill of health. Any reliable Portuguese Water Dog breeder should have a health certificate from a vet on all dogs for sale as well as documentation on relevant health testing on the parents (and pups, where applicable). If the breeder you select does not have the proper documentation, you should choose to look elsewhere.

Listed here are some of the more common health concerns that are known to affect the Portuguese Water Dog. It is hoped that a PWD is not affected by any of these conditions; nonetheless, potential buyers of the breed should be aware of all of these and discuss them with their chosen breeders.

COAT COLORS

The Portuguese Water Dog comes in several different colors. They are usually black with some shadings of white on the body. Other dogs may have various shades of brown, also some combinations of black or brown with white.

Hip Dysplasia

Canine hip dysplasia is a common disorder that can affect dogs of all sizes, although usually dogs that are medium to large in size. Hip dysplasia is a developmental defect in which the hip joint is improperly formed and, thus, the head of the femur does not fit correctly into the hip socket. It's absolutely essential that any Portuguese Water Dog that is being considered for breeding purposes have its hips x-rayed at two years of age. The Orthopedic Foundation for Animals assigns certification numbers to those dogs with non-dysplastic hips. Dogs that have not been granted OFA numbers should not be used for breeding. Even if the dog is not to be used in a breeding program, it might be best to have the hips checked anyway. It's always better to be safe than sorry.

Research has found that genetically pre-dysplastic dogs can be protected by restricting some environmental stress. There is even some indication that some puppy foods may speed up growth and therefore create a greater risk of the condition's developing. Allowing for stable and uniform growth is healthiest for the dog's development.

DELTA SOCIETY

The human-animal bond propels the work of the Delta Society, striving to improve the lives of people and animals. The Pet Partners Program proves that the lives of people and dogs are inextricably linked. The Pet Partners Program, a national registry, trains and screens volunteers for pet therapy in hospices, nursing homes, schools and rehabilitation centers. Dog-and-handler teams of Pet Partners volunteer in all 50 states, with nearly 7,000 teams making visits annually. About 900,000 patients, residents and students receive assistance each year. If you and your dog are interested in becoming Pet Partners, contact the Delta Society online at www.deltasociety.org.

Progressive Retinal Atrophy (PRA)

PRA is a condition in which the retinal cells degenerate, eventually causing the dog to go blind. It is a genetic disease that affects many breeds of dog. Statistics thus far indicate that the PWD is most commonly affected by late-onset PRA, with the majority of cases diagnosed in dogs 3 to 5 years of age or older. At first, affected dogs have difficulties seeing at night or in dim light. Eventually the disease can lead to total blindness.

Affected dogs can be detected by an electroretinogram at two years of age; methods of earlier detection have not yet been established. All dogs should have an annual examination. There is presently no clinical test to identify carriers of PRA, so carriers

Do You Know about Hip Dysplasia?

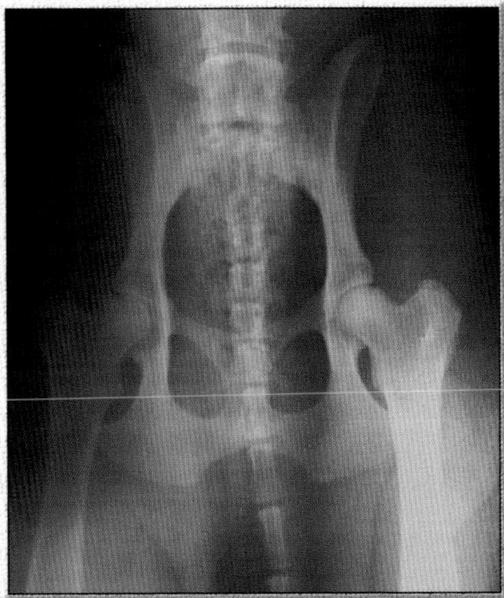

X-ray of a dog with "Good" hips.

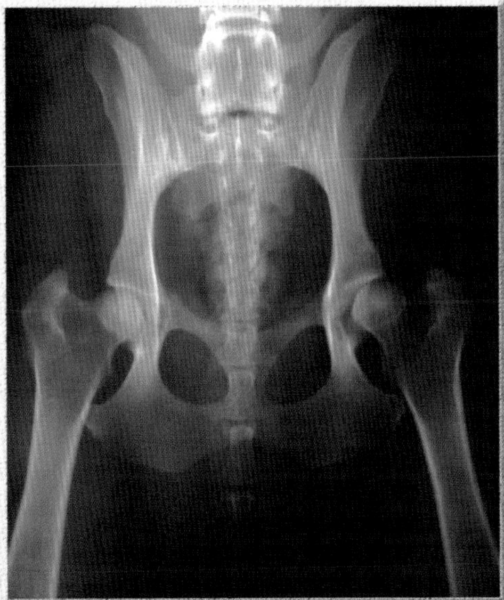

X-ray of a dog with "Moderate" dysplastic hips.

Hip dysplasia is a fairly common condition found in pure-bred dogs. When a dog has hip dysplasia, his hind leg has an incorrectly formed hip joint. By constant use of the hip joint, it becomes more and more loose, wears abnormally and may become arthritic.

Hip dysplasia can only be confirmed with an x-ray, but certain symptoms may indicate a problem. Your dog may have a hip dysplasia problem if he walks in a peculiar manner, hops instead of smoothly runs, uses his hind legs in unison (to keep the pressure off the weak joint), has trouble getting up from a prone position or always sits with both legs together on one side of his body.

As the dog matures, he may adapt well to life with a bad hip, but in a few years the arthritis develops and many dogs with hip dysplasia become crippled.

Hip dysplasia is considered an inherited disease and only can be diagnosed definitively by x-ray when the dog is two years old, although symptoms often appear earlier. Some experts claim that a special diet might help your puppy outgrow the bad hip, but the usual treatments are surgical. The removal of the pectineus muscle, the removal of the round part of the femur, reconstructing the pelvis and replacing the hip with an artificial one are all surgical interventions that are expensive, but they are usually very successful. Follow the advice of your veterinarian.

can only be accurately identified after they have produced offspring with PRA. Likewise, the offspring of an affected dog can be identified as carriers as well. It is recommended that all Portuguese Water Dog owners take their dogs for an annual ophthalmoscopic examination by a veterinary eye specialist.

STORAGE DISEASE

Storage disease (GM1 gangliosidosis) is a genetic condition in which the lack of an enzyme allows a build-up of toxic substances in the nerve cells. The gene for storage disease is recessive, so only Portuguese Water Dogs who obtain a defective gene from both parents are affected. A dog that has the disease will show signs of neurological deterioration and will die by six to eight months of age. A carrier of the disease will appear normal, but should not be bred.

OTHER HEALTH ISSUES

The health issues discussed here represent some of the most commonly seen in the PWD. Visit the PWDCA's website for an in-depth look at these and other problems, including heart disease (juvenile dilated cardiomyopathy being the most critical), renal dysplasia (causing kidney failure), cancer, seizure disorders, microphthalmia (an eye disorder) and allergies.

Puppies are usually tested at seven to eight weeks of age. There is no treatment or cure for the disease, but all indications are that breeders will eventually be able to eliminate the defective gene for storage disease from the Portuguese Water Dog gene pool.

ADDISON'S DISEASE

Signs of Addison's disease have been seen in young to middle-aged PWDs. It is caused by an adrenocortical hormone deficiency. Symptoms are rather generic, including lethargy, vomiting, diarrhea, lack of appetite and other signs that are not necessarily indicative of a serious condition. Thus Addison's may be misdiagnosed, but it will be fatal if not detected and treated. If symptoms persist, it is essential to have the veterinarian test the dog for Addison's disease, since it does occur in the Portuguese Water Dog. Treatment is through hormone-replacement therapy, usually for the rest of the dog's life. With treatment, an affected dog can live a normal life.

DISTICHIASIS

A dog affected by distichiasis may suffer from eye irritation caused by improperly located eyelashes. Although not yet established, it is probable that this is a hereditary condition; thus, incidences should be noted by breeders and discretion exercised in breeding affected dogs. The Portuguese Water Dog is one of a number of breeds in which distichiasis is present, and the condition can appear in a dog of any age.

Cataracts

A cataract is a lens opacity that may affect one or both eyes and may involve the partial or complete portion of the lens. It usually develops as a small white area and is hardly noticeable to the naked eye. A cataract can be a result of many different things, including heredity, trauma, inflammation and nutritional deficiencies. Although the exact occurrence of cataracts in the breed is not known, many older Portuguese Water Dogs develop cataracts. Fortunately, cataracts are readily amenable to surgical intervention with excellent results of restoring vision.

Follicular Dysplasia

One of the causes of hair loss in the PWD is follicular dysplasia, a genetic disorder. In the PWD, it is seen primarily in curly-coated dogs produced from two curly-coated parents. Loss of hair occurs on the chest, flanks, back, abdomen and around the rectum. Dogs that are afflicted with the disease will often show slight hair loss around one or both eyes when stressed. At the current time, there is no effective treatment. To eliminate follicular dysplasia, Portuguese Water Dog breeders recommend that curly-coated dogs be bred to wavy coats, not other curly coats.

The Portuguese Water Dog is, in general, a healthy and hardy breed with an average lifespan of 12 to 15 years.

BREED STANDARD FOR THE PORTUGUESE WATER DOG

WHAT IS A STANDARD?

All of the breeds currently recognized by the American Kennel Club for registration have a standard. The standard is written by the breed's parent club. The standard portrays what would be the ideal representative of the breed. The standard is not the representation of any actual dog, but simply a theory. The breed standard authorized by the American Kennel Club is used as a measuring stick by which AKC judges evaluate dogs at shows.

In a typical dog show, a judge will evaluate every competitor that is shown under him or her. The dog that most closely resembles the standard in the judge's determination is the dog that is placed first in the class. Not every judge will agree on which dog or dogs are best. That's what makes conformation competition exciting and appealing to the show dog aficionado. Each show features a different judging panel and completely different opinion as to which dogs best conform to the standard. The breed standard is the "blueprint" of the breed, the ideal for which every breeder strives.

The breed standard can be a very valuable asset for the novice and experienced dog owner, dog breeder and show judge. Any person interested in buying a puppy or adult PWD should study the breed standard thoroughly. It is a valuable guideline in determining the physical and tempera-

MEETING THE IDEAL

The American Kennel Club defines a standard as: "A description of the ideal dog of each recognized breed, to serve as an ideal against which dogs are judged at shows." This "blueprint" is drawn up by the breed's recognized parent club, approved by a majority of its membership and then submitted to the AKC for approval.

The AKC states that "An understanding of any breed must begin with its standard. This applies to all dogs, not just those intended for showing." The picture that the standard draws of the dog's type, gait, temperament and structure is the guiding image used by breeders as they plan their programs.

mental qualities that make up the Portuguese Water Dog, and some of the less desirable features (or faults) that you should be aware of before buying, even if selecting a pet-only dog. Although the perfect dog portrayed in the breed standard will likely never exist, it is in your best interest to attempt to obtain or breed a dog that closely resembles it.

THE AMERICAN KENNEL CLUB BREED STANDARD FOR THE PORTUGUESE WATER DOG

General Appearance: Known for centuries along Portugal's coast, this seafaring breed was prized by fishermen for a spirited, yet obedient nature, and a robust, medium build that allowed for a full day's work in and out of the water. The Portuguese Water Dog is a swimmer and diver of exceptional ability and stamina, who aided his master at sea by retrieving broken nets, herding schools of fish, and carrying messages between boats and to shore. He is a loyal companion and alert guard. This highly intelligent utilitarian breed is distinguished by two coat types, either curly or wavy; an impressive head of considerable breadth and well proportioned mass; a ruggedly built, well-knit body; and a powerful, thickly based tail, carried gallantly or used purposefully as a rudder. The Portuguese Water Dog provides an indelible impression of strength, spirit, and soundness.

"Spirited" and "attentive" are two adjectives from the breed standard that are aptly shown on this PWD's face.

Size, Proportion, Substance: *Size—Height* at the withers—Males, 20 to 23 inches. The ideal is 22 inches. Females, 17 to 21 inches. The ideal is 19 inches. *Weight*—For males, 42 to 60 pounds; for females, 35 to 50 pounds. *Proportion*—Off square; slightly longer than tall when

Head study—curly coat, retriever clip, showing correct substance, type and structure.

Dog in profile—wavy coat, lion clip. A self-colored dog showing correct type, proportion, structure and substance.

measured from prosternum to rearmost point of the buttocks, and from withers to ground. *Substance*—Strong, substantial bone; well developed, neither refined nor coarse, and a solidly built, muscular body.

Head: An essential characteristic; distinctively large, well proportioned and with exceptional breadth of topskull. *Expression*—Steady, penetrating, and attentive. *Eyes*— Medium in size; set well apart, and a bit obliquely. Roundish and neither prominent nor sunken. Black or various tones of brown in color. Darker eyes are preferred. Eye rims fully pigmented with black edges in black, black and white, or white dogs; brown edges in brown dogs. Haws are dark and not apparent. *Ears*—Set well above the line of the eye. Leather is heart shaped and thin. Except for a small opening at the back, ears are held nicely against the head. Tips should not reach below the lower jaw. *Skull*—In profile, it is slightly longer than the muzzle, its curvature more accentuated at the back than in the front. When viewed head-on, the top of the skull is very broad and appears domed, with a slight depression in the middle. The forehead is prominent, and has a central furrow, extending two-thirds of the distance from stop to occiput. The occiput is well defined. *Stop*—Well defined. *Muzzle*—Substantial; wider at the base than at the nose. *Jaws*—Strong and neither over nor undershot. *Nose*—Broad, well flared nostrils. Fully pigmented; black in dogs with black, black and white, or white coats; various tones of brown in dogs with brown coats. *Lips*—Thick, especially in front; no flew. Lips and mucous membranes of the roof of the mouth, under tongue, and gums are quite black, or well ticked with black in dogs with black, black and white, or white coats; various tones of brown in dogs with brown coats. *Bite*—Scissors or level. *Teeth*—Not visible when the mouth is closed. Canines strongly developed.

Neck, Topline, Body: *Neck*—Straight, short, round, and held high. Strongly muscled. No dewlap. *Topline*—Level and firm. *Body*—Chest is broad and deep, reaching down to the elbow. *Ribs* are long and well-sprung to provide optimum lung capacity. *Abdomen* well held up in a graceful line. *Back* is broad and well muscled. *Loin* is short and meets the croup smoothly. *Croup* is well formed and only slightly inclined with hip bones hardly apparent. *Tail*—Not docked; thick at the base and tapering; set on slightly below the line of the back; should not reach below the hock. When the dog is attentive the tail is held in a ring, the front of which should not reach forward of the loin. The tail is of great help when swimming and diving.

Forequarters: *Shoulders* are well inclined and very strongly muscled. *Upper arms* are strong. *Forelegs* are strong and straight with long, well muscled forearms. *Carpus* is heavy-boned, wider in front than at the side. *Pasterns* are long and strong. Dewclaws may be removed. *Feet* are round and rather flat. Toes neither knuckled up nor too long. Webbing between the toes is of soft skin, well covered with hair, and reaches the toe tips. Central pad is very thick, others normal. Nails held up slightly off the ground. Black, brown, white, and striped nails are allowed.

Thanks to the efforts of dedicated breeders and fanciers, the Portuguese Water Dog is generally hardy and long-lived—and he's certainly happy about it!

Hindquarters: Powerful; well balanced with the front assembly. *Legs*, viewed from the rear, are parallel to each other, straight and very strongly muscled in upper and lower thighs. *Buttocks* are well developed. *Tendons* and hocks are strong. *Metatarsus* long,

Dog in profile—curly coat, retriever clip. A parti-color dog showing correct type, proportion and substance.

FAULTS IN PROFILE (Retriever Clip)

Short thick neck, loaded shoulders, long back, lacking sufficient strength and angulation in the rear.

Upright shoulders, low on leg, soft topline, low tail set, lacking angulation behind.

no dewclaws. *Feet* similar in all respects to forefeet.

Coat: A profuse, thickly planted coat of strong, healthy hair, covering the whole body evenly, except where the forearm meets the brisket and in the groin area, where it is thinner. No undercoat, mane or ruff. There are *two varieties of coat: Curly*—Compact, cylindrical curls, somewhat lusterless. The hair on the ears is sometimes wavy. *Wavy*—Falling gently in waves, not curls, and with a slight sheen. *No preference will be given to coat type, either curly or wavy.*

Clip: Two clips are acceptable: *Lion Clip*—As soon as the coat grows long, the middle part and hindquarters, as well as the muzzle, are clipped. The hair at the end of the tail is left at full length. *Retriever Clip*—In order to give a natural appearance and a smooth unbroken line, the entire coat is scissored or clipped to follow the outline of the dog, leaving a short blanket of coat no longer than one inch in length. The hair at the end of the tail is left at full length. *No discrimination will be made against the correct presentation of a dog in either Lion Clip or Retriever Clip.*

Color: Black, white, and various tones of brown; also combinations of black or brown with white. A white coat does not imply albinism provided nose, mouth, and eyelids are black. In animals with black, white, or black and white coats, the skin is decidedly bluish.

Gait: Short, lively steps when walking. The trot is a forward striding, well balanced movement.

Temperament: An animal of spirited disposition, self-willed, brave, and very resistant to fatigue. A dog of exceptional intelligence and a loyal companion, it obeys its master with facility and apparent pleasure. It is obedient with those who look after it or with those for whom it works.

Summary Statement: The Portuguese Water Dog is spirited yet obedient, robust, and of unexaggerated, functional conformation; sure, substantially boned and muscled, and able to do a full day's work in and out of the water.

Faults: Any deviation from the described ideal is a fault. However, those inherent characteristics that are imperative for the maintenance of proper type, and therefore cannot be overlooked, are listed as Major Faults.

Major Faults:
1. *Temperament*—Shy, vicious, or unsound behavior.
2. *Head*—Unimpressive; small in overall size; narrow in topskull; snipy in muzzle.
3. *Substance*—Light or refined in bone; lacking in muscle.
4. *Coat*—Sparse; naturally short, close-lying hair, partially or over all; wispy or wiry in texture; brittle; double-coated.
5. *Tail*—Other than as described. Extremely low set. Heavy or droopy in action.
6. *Pigment*—Any deviation from described pigmentation; other than black or various tones of brown eye color; pink or partial pigmentation in nose, lips, eyes, or eye rims.
7. *Bite*—Overshot or undershot.

Approved January 15, 1991
Effective February 27, 1991

FAULTS IN PROFILE (Lion Clip)

Short neck, tail carried too tightly over back, lacking angulation in rear, high in the hock, weak flat feet.

Ewe-necked, upright shoulders, narrow front and toes out, long back, arch over loin, lacking strength and angulation in rear.

YOUR PUPPY

PORTUGUESE WATER DOG

WHERE TO BEGIN?

If you are convinced that the Portuguese Water Dog is the ideal dog for you, it's time to learn about where to find a puppy and what to look for. Although you may not find too many breeders who have a long standing in the breed, as the Portuguese Water Dog is still a relative youngster with regard to AKC recognition, you still must find a responsible breeder with outstanding dog ethics and a strong commitment to the breed. New owners should have as many questions as they have doubts. A dedicated breeder is indeed the one to answer your four million questions and make you comfortable with your choice of this enchanting breed, the Portuguese Water Dog.

When choosing a breeder, reputation is much more important than convenience of location. Choosing a breeder wisely is an important first step in dog ownership. Fortunately, the majority of Portuguese Water Dog breeders are devoted to the breed and its well-being. The AKC and Portuguese Water Dog Club of America (PWDCA) are trusted sources for breeder referrals. PWDCA member breeders are obliged to uphold a stringent code of ethics in their breeding programs. Potential owners are encouraged to attend dog shows (or agility trials or water-dog events) to see the Portuguese Water Dogs in action, to meet the owners and handlers firsthand and to get an idea of what PWDs look like outside a photographer's lens. Provided you approach the handlers when they are not busy with the dogs, most are more than willing to answer

THE FAMILY TREE

Your puppy's pedigree is his family tree. Just as a child may resemble his parents and grandparents, so too will a puppy reflect the qualities, good and bad, of his ancestors, especially those in the first two generations. Therefore, it's important to know as much as possible about a puppy's immediate relatives. Reputable and experienced breeders should be able to explain the pedigree and why they chose to breed from the particular dogs they used.

FINDING A QUALIFIED BREEDER

Before you begin your puppy search, ask for references from your veterinarian and perhaps other breeders to refer you to someone they believe is reputable. Responsible breeders usually raise only one or two breeds of dog. Avoid any breeder who has several different breeds or has several litters at the same time. Dedicated breeders are usually involved with a breed or other dog club. Many participate in some sport or activity related to their breed. Just as you want to be assured of the breeder's qualifications, the breeder wants to be assured that you will make a worthy owner. Expect the breeder to interview you, asking questions about your goals for the pup, your experience with dogs and what kind of home you will provide.

questions, recommend breeders and give advice.

Once you have contacted and met a breeder or two and made your choice about which breeder is best suited to your needs, it's time to visit the litter. Don't be surprised if the breeders have waiting lists. Sometimes new owners have to wait over a year for a puppy. If you are really committed to the breeder whom you've selected, then you will wait. If you've done your homework and chosen the breeder with care, your wait will be worth it!

Breeders commonly allow visitors to see the litter by around the fifth or sixth week, and puppies leave for their new homes between the eighth and tenth week. Breeders who permit their puppies to leave early are more interested in a profit than their puppies' well-being. Puppies need to learn the rules of the pack from their dams, and most dams continue teaching the pups manners and dos and don'ts until at least the eighth week. Breeders spend significant amounts of time with the Portuguese Water Dog toddlers so that they are able to interact with the "other species," i.e. humans. Given the long history that dogs and humans have, bonding between the two species is natural but must be nurtured. A well-bred, well-socialized Portuguese Water Dog pup wants nothing more than to be near you and please you.

Pet or show dog? The choice is up to you. However, whatever your intentions for your Portuguese Water Dog, a reputable breeder is the best person to supply a pup.

SIGNS OF A HEALTHY PUPPY

Healthy puppies are robust little fellows who are alert and active, sporting shiny coats and supple skin. They should not appear lethargic, bloated or pot-bellied, nor should they have flaky skin or runny or crusted eyes or noses. Their stools should be firm and well formed, with no evidence of blood or mucus.

Always check the bite of your selected puppy to be sure that it is neither overshot nor undershot. Often a poor bite corrects itself as the puppy ages, but if you are selecting a show dog, this is not a wise risk to take.

You are advised not to forget, in your enthusiasm, to inquire about the common diseases in the breed and health problems that the breeder has encountered in his line. The health of a puppy is the most important consideration when selecting a dog of any breed.

A COMMITTED NEW OWNER

By now you should understand what makes the PWD a most unique and special dog, one that may fit nicely into your family and lifestyle. If you have researched breeders, you should be able to recognize a knowledgeable and responsible PWD breeder who cares not only about his pups but also about what kind of owner you will be. If you have completed the final step in your new journey, you have found a litter, or possibly two, of quality PWD pups.

A visit with the puppies and their breeder should be an education in itself. Breed research, breeder selection and puppy visitation are very important aspects of finding the puppy of your dreams. Beyond that, these things also lay the foundation for a successful future with your pup. Puppy personalities within each litter vary, from the shy and easygoing puppy to the one who is dominant and assertive, with most pups falling somewhere in between. By spending time with the puppies, you will be able to recognize certain behaviors and what these behaviors indicate about each pup's temperament. Which type of pup will complement your family dynamics is best determined by observing the puppies in action within their "pack." Your breeder's expertise and recommendations are also valuable. Although you may fall in love with a bold and brassy male, the breeder may suggest that another pup would be best for you. The breeder's experience in rearing PWD pups and matching their temperaments with appropriate humans offers the best assurance that your pup will meet your needs and expectations. The type of puppy that you select is just as important as your decision that the PWD is the breed for you.

The decision to live with a PWD is a serious commitment and not one to be taken lightly. This puppy is a living sentient being that will be dependent on you for basic survival for his entire life. Beyond the basics of survival—food, water, shelter and protection—he needs much, much more. The new pup needs love, nurturing and a proper canine education to mold him into a responsible, well-behaved canine citizen. Your PWD's health and good manners will need consistent monitoring and regular "tune-ups," so your job as a responsible dog owner will be ongoing throughout every stage of his life. If you are not prepared to accept these responsibilities and commit to them for the next decade, likely longer, then you are not prepared to own a dog of any breed.

Although the responsibilities of owning a dog may at times tax

HEART-HEALTHY

In this modern age of ever-improving cardio-care, no doctor or scientist can dispute the advantages of owning a dog to lower a person's risk of heart disease. Studies have proven that petting a dog, walking a dog and grooming a dog all show positive results toward lowering your blood pressure. The simple routine of exercising your dog—going outside with the dog and walking, jogging or playing catch—is heart-healthy in and of itself. If you are normally less active than your physician thinks you should be, adopting a dog may be a smart option to improve your own quality of life as well as that of another creature.

your patience, the joy of living with your PWD far outweighs the workload, and a well-mannered adult dog is worth your time and effort. Before your very eyes, your new charge will grow up to be your most loyal friend, devoted to you unconditionally.

YOUR PWD SHOPPING LIST

Just as expectant parents prepare a nursery for their baby, so should you ready your home for the arrival of your PWD pup. If you have the necessary puppy supplies purchased and in place before he comes home, it will ease the puppy's transition from the warmth and familiarity of his mom and littermates to the brand-new environment of his new home and human family. You will be too busy to stock up and prepare your house after your pup comes home, that's for sure! Imagine how a pup must feel upon being transported to a strange new place. It's up to you to comfort him and to let your little PWD pup know that he is going to be happy with you.

GETTING ACQUAINTED

When visiting a litter, ask the breeder for suggestions on how best to interact with the puppies. If possible, get right into the middle of the pack and sit down with them. Observe which pups climb into your lap and which ones shy away. Toss a toy for them to chase and bring back to you. It's easy to fall in love with the puppy who picks you, but keep your future objectives in mind before you make your final decision.

Food and Water Bowls

Your puppy will need separate bowls for his food and water. Stainless steel pans are generally preferred over plastic bowls since they sterilize better and pups are less inclined to chew on the metal. Heavy-duty ceramic bowls are popular, but consider how often you will have to pick up those heavy bowls. Buy adult-sized pans, as your puppy will grow into them before your eyes.

The Dog Crate

If you think that crates are tools of punishment and confinement for when a dog has misbehaved, think again. Most breeders and almost all trainers recommend a crate as the preferred house-training aid as well as for all-around puppy training and safety. Because dogs are natural den creatures that prefer cave-like environments, the benefits of crate use are many. The crate provides the puppy with his very own "safe house," a cozy place to sleep, take a break or seek comfort with a favorite toy; a travel aid to house your dog when on the road, at motels or at the vet's office; a training aid to help teach your puppy proper toileting habits; a place of solitude when non-dog people happen to drop by and don't want a lively puppy—or even a well-behaved adult dog—saying hello or begging for attention.

Crates come in several types, although the wire crate and the fiberglass airline-type crate are the most popular. Both are safe and your puppy will adjust to

ABOVE: At seven-and-a-half weeks old, these pups only have a short while to go before they will be ready for their new homes. **BELOW:** Mom and pup have dinner together. The pup is used to doing everything with his canine pack before he makes the transition to a human pack.

PEDIGREE VS. REGISTRATION CERTIFICATE

Too often new owners are confused between these two important documents. Your puppy's pedigree, essentially a family tree, is a written record of a dog's genealogy of three generations or more. The pedigree will show you the names as well as performance titles of all dogs in your pup's background. Your breeder must provide you with a registration application, with his part properly filled out. You must complete the application and send it to the AKC with the proper fee. Every puppy must come from a litter that has been AKC-registered by the breeder, born in the US and from a sire and dam that are also registered with the AKC.

The seller must provide you with complete records to identify the puppy. The AKC requires that the seller provide the buyer with the following: breed; sex, color and markings; date of birth; litter number (when available); names and registration numbers of the parents; breeder's name; and date sold or delivered.

Three different crate types: mesh (LEFT), wire (RIGHT) and fiberglass (TOP).

either one, so the choice is up to you. The wire crates offer better visibility for the pup as well as better ventilation and are the more popular choice for use in the home. Many of the wire crates easily fold down for easy transport. The fiberglass crates, similar to those used by the airlines for animal transport, are sturdier and more den-like. However, the fiberglass crates do not collapse and are less ventilated than a wire crate, which can be problematic in hot weather. Some of the newer crates are made of heavy plastic mesh; they are very lightweight and fold up into slim-line suitcases. However, a mesh crate might not be suitable for a pup with manic chewing habits.

Don't bother with a puppy-sized crate. Although your PWD will be a wee fellow when you bring him home, he will grow up in the blink of an eye and your puppy crate will be useless. Purchase a crate that will accommodate an adult PWD. A large crate, measuring about 42 inches long by 28 inches wide by 31 inches high, should suit him nicely.

Bedding and Crate Pads

Your puppy will enjoy some type of soft bedding in his "room" (the crate), something he can snuggle into to feel cozy and secure. Old towels or blankets are good choices for a young pup, since he may (and probably will) have a toileting accident or two in the

CRATE EXPECTATIONS

To make the crate more inviting to your puppy, you can offer his first meal or two inside the crate, always keeping the crate door open so that he does not feel confined. Keep a favorite toy or two in the crate for him to play with while inside. You can also cover the crate at night with a lightweight sheet to make it more den-like and remove the stimuli of household activity. Never put him into his crate as punishment or as you are scolding him, since he will then associate his crate with negative situations and avoid going there.

crate or decide to chew on the bedding material. Once he is fully trained and out of the early chewing stage, you can replace the puppy bedding with a permanent crate pad if you prefer. Crate pads and other dog beds run the gamut from inexpensive to high-end doggie-designer styles, but don't splurge on the good stuff until you are sure that your puppy is reliable and won't tear it up or make a mess on it.

A crate pad lining a wire crate creates a comfy "home-within-a-home" for a dog.

Puppy Toys

Just as infants and older children require objects to stimulate their minds and bodies, puppies need toys to entertain their curious brains, wiggly paws and achy teeth. A fun array of safe doggie toys will help satisfy your puppy's chewing instincts and distract him from gnawing on the leg of your antique chair or your new leather sofa. Most puppy toys are cute and look as if they would be a lot of fun, but not all are necessarily safe or good for your puppy, so use caution when you go puppy-toy shopping.

Although PWDs are not known to be voracious chewers, they still, like most dogs, love to chew. The best "chewcifiers" are nylon and hard rubber bones which are safe to gnaw on and come in sizes appropriate for all age groups and breeds. Be especially careful of natural bones, which can splinter or develop dangerous sharp edges; pups can easily swallow or choke on those bone splinters. Veterinarians often tell of surgical nightmares involving bits of splintered bone, because in addition to the danger of choking, the sharp pieces can damage the intestinal tract.

COST OF OWNERSHIP

The purchase price of your puppy is merely the first expense in the typical dog budget. Quality dog food, veterinary care (sickness and health maintenance), dog supplies and grooming costs will add up to big bucks every year. Can you adequately afford to support a canine addition to the family?

TOYS 'R SAFE

The vast array of tantalizing puppy toys is staggering. Stroll through any pet shop or pet-supply outlet and you will see that the choices can be overwhelming. However, not all dog toys are safe or sensible. Most very young puppies enjoy soft woolly toys that they can snuggle with and carry around. (You know they have outgrown them when they shred them up!) Avoid toys that have buttons, tabs or other enhancements that can be chewed off and swallowed. Soft toys that squeak are fun, but make sure your puppy does not disembowel the toy and remove (and swallow) the squeaker. Toys that rattle or make noise can excite a puppy, but they present the same danger as the squeaky kind and so require supervision. Hard rubber toys that bounce can also entertain a pup, but make sure that the toy is too big for your pup to swallow.

Similarly, rawhide chews, while a favorite of most dogs and puppies, can be equally dangerous. Pieces of rawhide are easily swallowed after they get soft and gummy from chewing, and dogs have been known to choke on large pieces of ingested rawhide. Rawhide chews should be offered only when you can supervise the puppy.

Soft woolly toys are special puppy favorites. They come in a wide variety of cute shapes and sizes; some look like little stuffed animals. Puppies love to shake them up and toss them about, or simply carry them around. Be careful of fuzzy toys that have button eyes or noses that your pup could chew off and swallow, and make sure that he does not disembowel a squeaky toy to remove the squeaker! Braided rope toys are similar in that they are fun to chew and toss around, but they shred easily and the strings are easy to swallow. The strings are not digestible and, if the puppy doesn't pass them in his stool, he could end up at the vet's office. As with rawhides, your puppy should be closely monitored with rope toys.

If you believe that your pup has ingested one of these forbidden objects, check his stools for the next couple of days to see if he passes them when he defecates. At the same time, also watch for signs of intestinal distress. A call to your veterinarian might be in order to get his advice and be on the safe side.

An all-time favorite toy for puppies (young and old!) is the empty gallon milk jug. Hard plastic juice containers—46 ounces or more—are also excellent. Such containers make lots of noise when they are batted about, and puppies go crazy with delight as they play with them. However, they don't last very long, so be sure to remove and replace them when they get chewed up.

A word of caution about homemade toys: be careful with your choices of non-traditional play objects. Never use old shoes or socks, since a puppy cannot distinguish between the old ones on which he's allowed to chew and the new ones in your closet that are strictly off limits. That principle applies to anything that resembles something that you don't want your puppy to chew.

TEETHING TIME

All puppies chew. It's normal canine behavior. Chewing just plain feels good to a puppy, especially during the three- to five-month teething period when the adult teeth are breaking through the gums. Rather than attempting to eliminate such a strong natural chewing instinct, you will be more successful if you redirect it and teach your puppy what he may or may not chew. Correct inappropriate chewing with a sharp "No!" and offer him a chew toy, praising him when he takes it. Don't become discouraged. Chewing usually decreases after the adult teeth have come in.

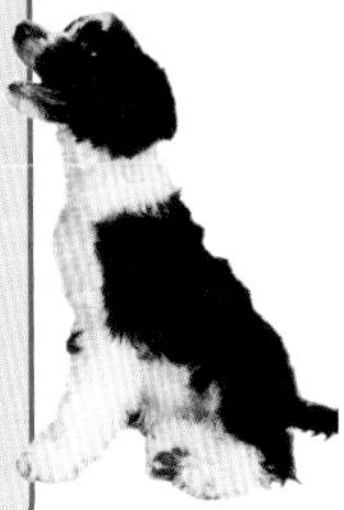

COLLARS

A lightweight nylon collar is the best choice for a very young pup. Quick-clip collars are easy to put on and remove, and they can be adjusted as the puppy grows. Introduce him to his collar as soon as he comes home to get him accustomed to wearing it. He'll get used to it quickly and won't mind a bit. Make sure that it is snug enough that it won't slip off, yet loose enough to be comfortable for the pup. You should be able to slip two fingers between the collar and his neck. Check the collar often, as puppies grow in spurts, and his collar can become too tight almost overnight. Choke collars are not recommended for the PWD. Not only can this type of collar damage the breed's coat, but it can be too harsh a training device for the sensitive PWD, who does best with positive methods.

LEASHES

A 6-foot nylon lead is an excellent choice for a young puppy. It is lightweight and not as tempting to chew as a leather lead. You can switch to a 6-foot leather lead after your pup has grown and is used to walking politely on a lead. For initial puppy walks and house-training purposes, you should invest in a shorter lead so that you have more control over the puppy. At first, you don't want him wandering too far away from you, and when taking him out for toileting you will want to keep him in the specific area chosen for his potty spot.

Once the puppy is heel-trained with a traditional leash, you can consider purchasing a retractable lead. This type of lead is excellent for walking adult dogs that are already leash-wise. The retractable lead allows the dog to roam farther away from you and explore a wider area when out walking, and also retracts when you need to keep him close to you.

Some breeders give owners a head start with crate training by acclimating their pups to crates before they go to new homes.

Your PWD will have fun with his toys—even more fun if you play with him!

HOME SAFETY FOR YOUR PUPPY

The importance of puppy-proofing cannot be overstated. In addition to making your house comfortable for your PWD's arrival, you also must make sure that your house is safe for your puppy before you bring him home. There are countless hazards in the owner's personal living environment that a pup can sniff, chew, swallow or destroy. Many are obvious; others are not. Do a thorough advance house check to remove or rearrange those things that could hurt your puppy, keeping any potentially dangerous items out of areas to which he will have access.

Electrical cords are especially dangerous, since puppies view them as irresistible chew toys. Unplug and remove all exposed cords or fasten them beneath a baseboard where the puppy cannot reach them. Veterinarians

Collaring Our Canines

The standard flat collar with a buckle or a snap, in leather, nylon or cotton, is widely regarded as the everyday all-purpose collar. If the collar fits correctly, you should be able to fit two fingers between the collar and the dog's neck.

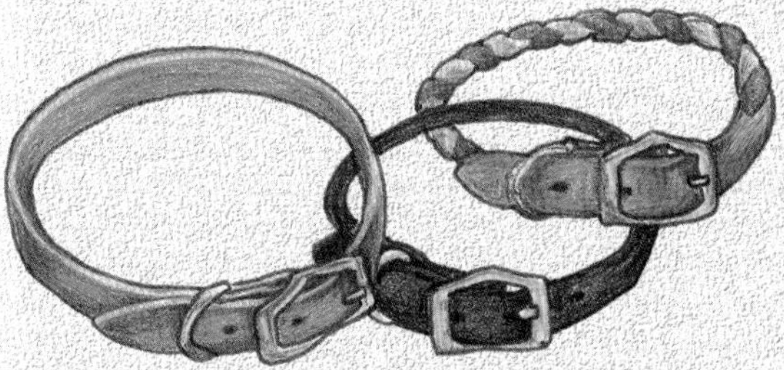

Leather Buckle Collars

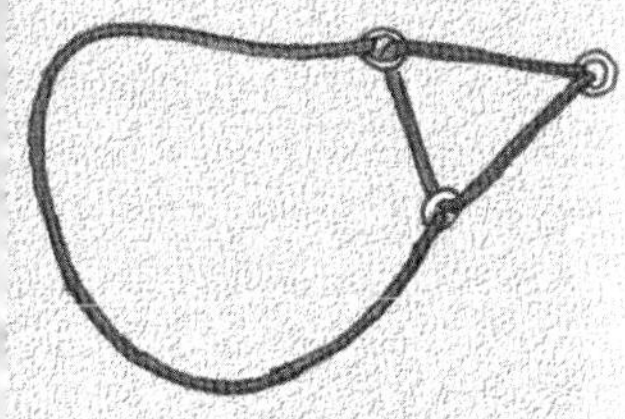

Limited-Slip Collar

The martingale, Greyhound or limited-slip collar is preferred by many dog owners and trainers. It is fixed with an extra loop that tightens when pressure is applied to the leash. The martingale collar gets tighter but does not "choke" the dog. The limited-slip collar should only be used for walking and training, not for free play or interaction with another dog. These types of collar should never be left on the dog, as the extra loop can lead to accidents.

Choke collars, usually made of stainless steel, are made for training purposes, though are not recommended for small dogs or heavily coated breeds. The chains can injure small dogs or damage long/abundant coats. Thin nylon choke leads are commonly used on show dogs while in the ring, though they are not practical for everyday use.

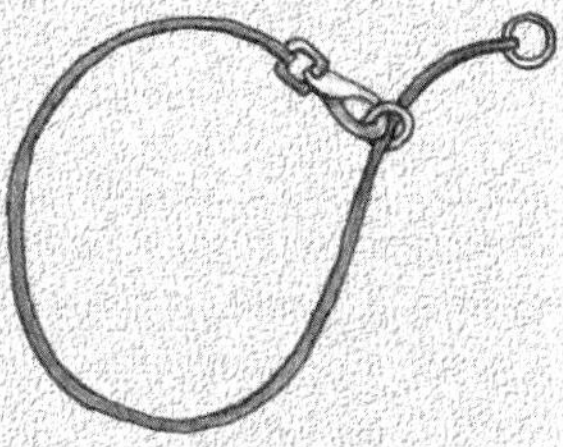

Snap Bolt Choke Collar

The harness, with two or three straps that attach over the dog's shoulders and around his torso, is a humane and safe alternative to the conventional collar. By and large, a well-made harness is virtually escape-proof. Harnesses are available in nylon and mesh and can be outfitted on most dogs, with chest girths ranging from 10 to 30 inches.

Harness

Nylon Collar

Quick-Click Closure

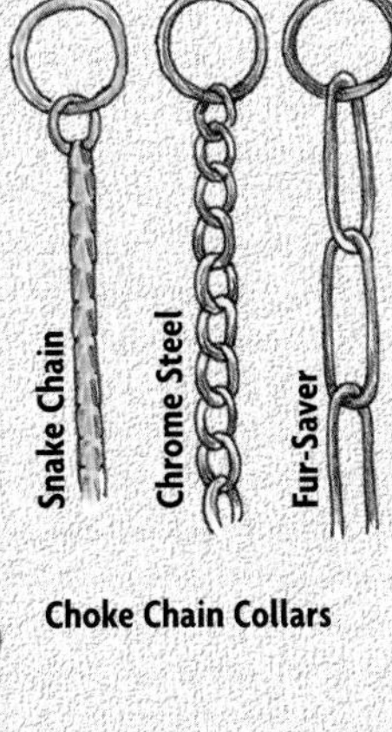

Choke Chain Collars

A head collar, composed of a nylon strap that goes around the dog's muzzle and a second strap that wraps around his neck, offers the owner better control over his dog. This device is recommended for problem-solving with dogs (including jumping up, pulling and aggressive behaviors), but must be used with care.

A training halter, including a flat collar and two straps, made of nylon and webbing, is designed for walking. There are several on the market; some are more difficult to put on the dog than others. The halter harness, with two small slip rings at each end, is recommended for ease of use.

Leash Life

Dogs love leashes! Believe it or not, most dogs dance for joy every time their owners pick up their leashes. The leash means that the dog is going for a walk—and there are few things more exciting than that! Here are some of the kinds of leashes that are commercially available.

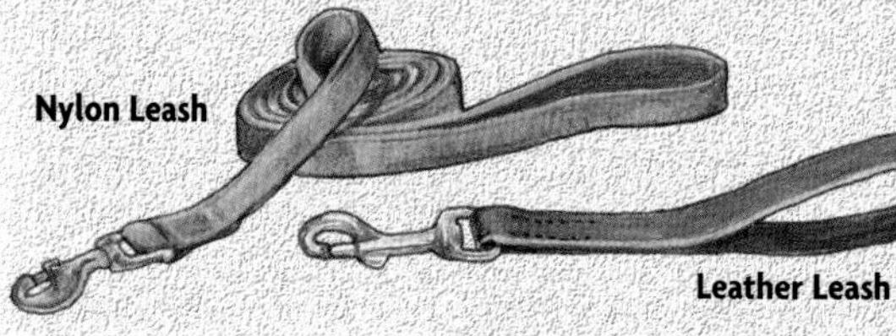

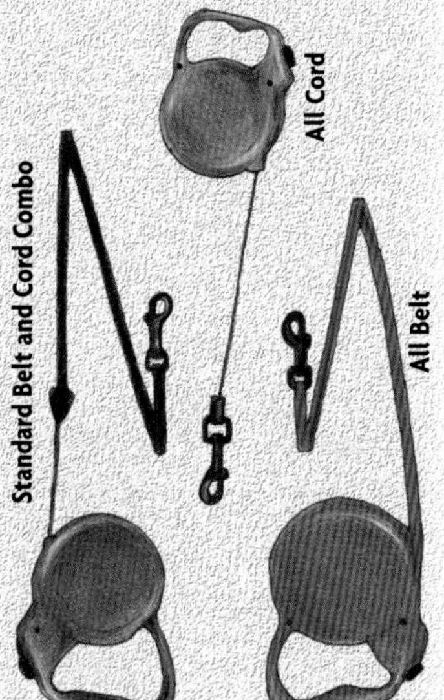

Retractable Leashes

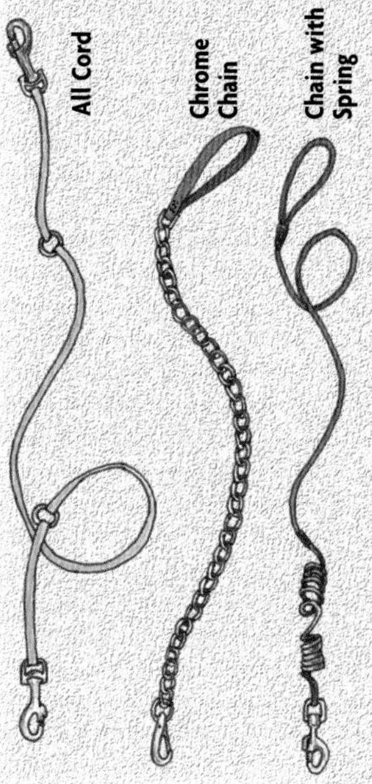

Traditional Leash: Made of cotton, nylon or leather, these leashes are usually about 6 feet in length. A quality-made leather leash is softer on the hands than a nylon one. Durable woven cotton is a popular option. Lengths can vary up to about 48 feet, designed for different uses.

Chain Leash: Usually a metal chain leash with a plastic handle. This is not the best choice for most breeds, as it is heavier than other leashes and difficult to manage.

Retractable Leash: A long nylon cord is housed in a plastic device for extending and retracting. This leash is ideal for taking trained dogs for long walks in open areas, although it is not recommended for large, powerful breeds. Different lengths and sizes are available, so check that you purchase one appropriate for your dog's weight.

Elastic Leash: A nylon leash with an elastic extension. This is useful for well-trained dogs, especially in conjunction with a head halter. Avoid leashes that are completely elastic, as they afford minimal control to the handler.

Adjustable Leash: This has two snaps, one on each end, and several metal rings. It is handy if you need to tether your dog temporarily, but is never to be used with a choke collar.

Tab Leash: A short leash (4 to 6 inches long) that attaches to your dog's collar. This device serves like a handle, in case you have to grab your dog while he's exercising off lead. It's ideal for "half-trained" dogs or dogs that listen only half the time.

Slip Leash: Essentially a leash with a collar built in, similar to what a dog-show handler uses to show a dog. This British-style collar has a ring on the end so that you can form a slip collar. Useful if you have to catch your own runaway dog or a stray.

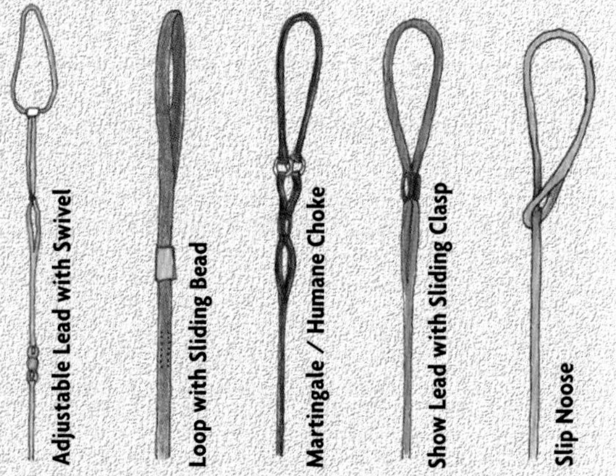

A Variety of Collar and-Leash-in-One Products

and firefighters can tell you horror stories about electrical burns and house fires that resulted from puppy-chewed electrical cords. Consider this a most serious precaution for your puppy and the rest of your family.

Scout your home for tiny objects that might be seen at a pup's eye level. Keep medication bottles and cleaning supplies well out of reach, and do the same with waste baskets and other trash containers. It goes without saying that you should not use rodent poison or other toxic chemicals in any puppy area and that you must keep such containers safely locked up. You will be amazed at how many places a curious puppy can discover!

Once your house has cleared inspection, check your yard. A sturdy fence, will give your dog a safe place to play and potty.

The great outdoors and a favorite toy—all that's missing is a friend to play with!

Although PWDs aren't known for being escape artists, they are still athletic dogs, so a 5- to 6-foot-high fence, well embedded into the ground to prevent digging out, will be necessary to contain an agile youngster or adult. Check the fence periodically for

CONFINEMENT

It is wise to keep your puppy confined to a small "puppy-proofed" area of the house for his first few weeks at home. Gate or block off a space near the door he will use for outdoor potty trips. Expandable baby gates are useful to create puppy's designated area. If he is allowed to roam through the entire house or even only several rooms, it will be more difficult to house-train him.

A Dog-Safe Home

The dog-safety police are taking you and your new puppy on a house tour. Let's go room by room and see how safe your own home is for your new pup. The following items are doggie dangers, so either they must be removed or the dog should be monitored or not have access to these areas.

Living Room

- house plants (some varieties are poisonous)
- fireplace or wood-burning stove
- paint on the walls (lead-based paint is toxic)
- lead drapery weights (toxic lead)
- lamps and electrical cords
- carpet cleaners or deodorizers

Outdoor

- swimming pool
- pesticides
- toxic plants
- lawn fertilizers

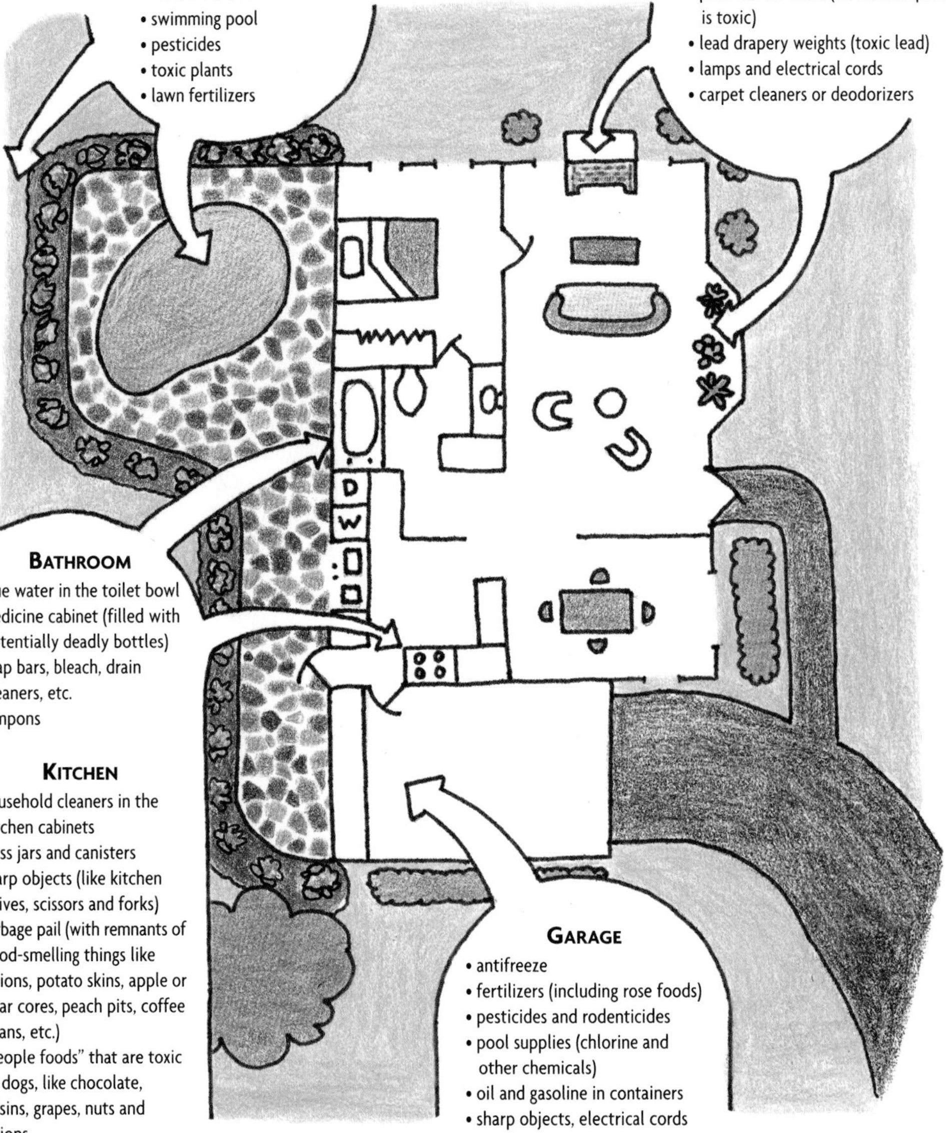

Bathroom

- blue water in the toilet bowl
- medicine cabinet (filled with potentially deadly bottles)
- soap bars, bleach, drain cleaners, etc.
- tampons

Kitchen

- household cleaners in the kitchen cabinets
- glass jars and canisters
- sharp objects (like kitchen knives, scissors and forks)
- garbage pail (with remnants of good-smelling things like onions, potato skins, apple or pear cores, peach pits, coffee beans, etc.)
- "people foods" that are toxic to dogs, like chocolate, raisins, grapes, nuts and onions

Garage

- antifreeze
- fertilizers (including rose foods)
- pesticides and rodenticides
- pool supplies (chlorine and other chemicals)
- oil and gasoline in containers
- sharp objects, electrical cords and power tools

necessary repairs. If there is a weak link or space to squeeze through, you can be sure a determined PWD will discover it.

The garage and shed can be hazardous places for a pup, as things like fertilizers, chemicals and tools are usually kept there. It's best to keep these areas off limits to the pup. Antifreeze is especially dangerous to dogs, as they find the taste appealing and it takes only a few licks from the driveway to kill a dog, puppy or adult, small breed or large.

VISITING THE VETERINARIAN

A good veterinarian is your PWD puppy's best health-insurance policy. If you do not already have a vet, ask friends and experienced dog people in your area for recommendations so that you can select a vet before you bring your PWD puppy home. Also arrange for your puppy's first veterinary examination beforehand, since many vets will not have appointments available immediately when you call and your puppy should visit the vet within a day or so of coming home.

It's important to make sure your puppy's first visit to the vet is a pleasant and positive one. The vet should take great care to befriend the pup and handle him gently to make their first meeting a positive experience. The vet will give the pup a thorough physical examination and set up

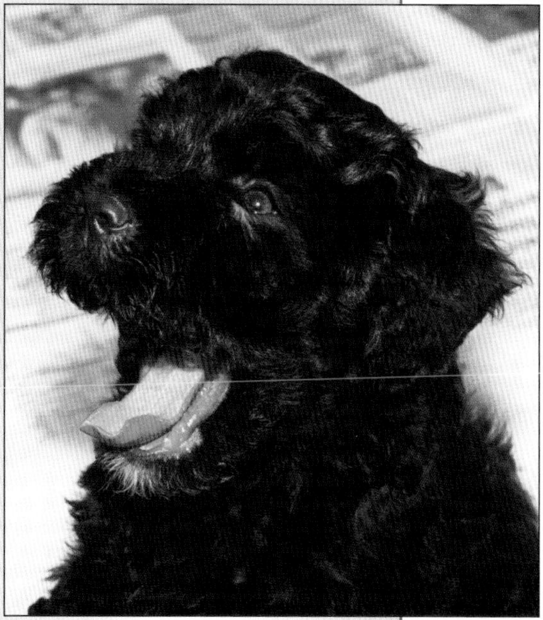

ASK THE VET

Help your vet help you to become a well-informed dog owner. Don't be shy about becoming involved in your puppy's veterinary care by asking questions and gaining as much knowledge as you can. For starters, ask what shots your puppy is getting and what diseases they prevent, and discuss with your vet the safest way to vaccinate. Find out what is involved in your dog's annual wellness visits. If you plan to spay or neuter, discuss the best age at which to have this done. Start out on the right "paw" with your puppy's vet and develop good communication with him, as he will care for your dog's health throughout the dog's entire life.

Too tired to eat? A puppy's first day at home will be exhausting for him, and he will definitely need time to rest and wind down from the excitement.

a schedule for vaccinations and other necessary wellness visits. Be sure to show your vet any health and inoculation records, which you should have received from your breeder. Your vet is a great source of canine health information, so be sure to ask questions and take notes. Creating a health journal for your puppy will make a handy reference for his wellness and any future health problems that may arise.

PUPPY PARASITES

Parasites are nasty little critters that live in or on your dog or puppy. Most puppies are born with ascarid roundworms, which are acquired from dormant ascarids residing in the dam. Other parasites can be acquired through contact with infected fecal matter. Take a stool sample to your vet for testing. He will prescribe a safe wormer to treat any parasites found in your puppy's stool. Always have a fecal test performed at your puppy's annual veterinary exam.

MEETING THE FAMILY

Your PWD's homecoming is an exciting time for all members of the family, and it's only natural that everyone will be eager to meet him, pet him and play with him. However, for the puppy's sake, it's best to make these initial family meetings as uneventful as possible so that the pup is not overwhelmed with too much too soon. Remember, he has just left his dam and his littermates and is away from the breeder's home for the first time. Despite his constantly wagging tail, he is still apprehensive and wondering where he is and who all these strange humans are. It's best to let him explore on his own and meet the family members as he feels comfortable. Let him investigate all the new smells, sights and sounds at his own pace. Children should be especially careful to not get overly excited, use loud voices or hug the pup too tightly. Be calm, gentle and affectionate, and be ready to comfort him if he appears frightened or uneasy.

Be sure to show your puppy his new crate during this first day home. Toss a treat or two inside the crate; if he associates the crate with food, he will associate the crate with good things. If he is comfortable with the crate, you can offer him his first meal inside it. Leave the door ajar so he can wander in and out as he chooses.

FIRST NIGHT IN HIS NEW HOME

So much has happened in your PWD puppy's first day away from the breeder. He's had his first car ride to his new home. He's met his new human family and perhaps the other family pets. He has explored his new house and yard, at least those places where he is to be allowed during his first weeks at home. He may have visited his new veterinarian. He has eaten his first meal or two away from his dam and littermates. Surely that's enough to tire out an eight-week-old PWD pup…or so you hope!

It's bedtime. During the day, the pup investigated his crate, which is his new den and sleeping space, so it is not entirely strange to him. Line the crate with a soft towel or blanket that he can snuggle into and gently place him into the crate for the night. Some breeders send home a piece of bedding from where the pup slept with his littermates, and those familiar scents are a great comfort for the puppy on his first night without his siblings.

He will probably whine or cry. The puppy is objecting to the confinement and the fact that he is alone for the first time. This can be a stressful time for you as well as for the pup. It's important that you remain strong and don't let the puppy out of his crate to comfort him. He will fall asleep eventually. If you release him, the puppy will learn that crying means "out" and will continue that habit. You are laying the groundwork for future habits.

TOXIC PLANTS

Plants are natural puppy magnets, but many can be harmful, even fatal, if ingested by a puppy or adult dog. Scout your yard and home interior and remove any plants, bushes or flowers that could be even mildly dangerous. It could save your puppy's life. You can obtain a complete list of toxic plants from your veterinarian, at the public library or by looking online.

The PWD should be a happy, friendly dog who enjoys life—and it should show!

Some breeders find that soft music can soothe a crying pup and help him get to sleep.

SOCIALIZING YOUR PUPPY

The first 20 weeks of your PWD puppy's life are the most important of his entire lifetime. A properly socialized puppy will grow up to be a confident and stable adult who will be a pleasure to live with and a welcome addition to the neighborhood.

The importance of socialization cannot be overemphasized. Research on canine behavior has proven that puppies who are not exposed to new sights, sounds, people and animals during their first 20 weeks of life will grow up to be timid and fearful, even aggressive, and unable to flourish outside of their familiar home environment.

Socializing your puppy is not difficult and, in fact, will be a fun time for you both. Lead training goes hand in hand with socialization, so your puppy will be learning how to walk on a lead at the same time that he's meeting the neighborhood. Because the PWD is such a terrific breed, people will want to meet him and your puppy will enjoy being "the new kid on the block." Take him for short walks, to the park and to other dog-friendly places where he will encounter new people, especially children. Puppies automatically recognize children as "little people" and are drawn to play

WATCH THE WATER

To help your puppy sleep through the night without having to relieve himself, remove his water bowl after 7 p.m. Offer him a couple of ice cubes during the evening to quench his thirst. Never leave water in a puppy's crate, as this is inviting puddles of mishaps.

with them. Just make sure that you supervise these meetings and that the children do not get too rough or encourage him to play too hard. PWDs are good with children, but in his excitement an overzealous pup can often nip too hard, frightening the child and in turn making the puppy overly excited. A bad experience in puppyhood can impact a dog for life, so a pup that has a negative experience with a child may grow up to be shy or even aggressive around children.

Take your puppy along on your daily errands. Puppies are natural "people magnets," and most people who see your pup will want to pet him. All of these encounters will help to mold him into a confident adult dog. Likewise, you will soon feel like a confident, responsible dog owner, rightly proud of your handsome PWD.

Be especially careful of your puppy's encounters and experiences during the eight-to-ten-week-old period, which is also called the "fear period." This is a serious imprinting period, and all contact during this time should be gentle and positive. A frightening or negative event could leave a permanent impression that could affect his future behavior if a similar situation arises.

Also make sure that your puppy has received his first and second rounds of vaccinations before you expose him to other dogs or bring him to places that other dogs may frequent. Avoid dog parks and other strange-dog

BE CONSISTENT

Consistency is a key element, in fact is absolutely necessary, to a puppy's learning environment. A behavior (such as chewing, jumping up or climbing onto the furniture) cannot be forbidden one day and then allowed the next. That will only confuse the pup, and he will not understand what he is supposed to do. Just one or two episodes of allowing an undesirable behavior to "slide" will imprint that behavior on a puppy's brain and make that behavior more difficult to erase or change.

areas until your vet assures you that your puppy is fully immunized and resistant to the diseases that can be passed between canines. Discuss socialization with your breeder, as some breeders recommend socializing the puppy even before he has received all of his inoculations, depending on how outgoing the puppy may be.

LEADER OF THE PUPPY'S PACK

Like other canines, your puppy needs an authority figure, someone he can look up to and regard as the leader of his "pack." His first pack leader was his dam, who taught him to be polite and not chew too hard on her ears or nip at her muzzle. He learned those same lessons from his littermates. If he played too rough, they cried in pain and stopped the game, which sent an important message to the rowdy puppy.

As puppies play together, they are also struggling to determine who will be the boss. Being pack animals, dogs need someone to be in charge. If a litter of puppies remained together beyond puppyhood, one of the pups would emerge as the strongest one, the one who calls the shots.

Once your puppy leaves the pack, he will look intuitively for a new leader. If he does not recognize you as that leader, he will try to assume that position for himself. Of course, it is hard to imagine your adorable PWD puppy trying to be in charge when he is so small and seemingly helpless. You must remember that these are natural canine instincts. Do not cave in and allow your pup to get the upper "paw"!

Just as socialization is so important during these first 20 weeks, so too is your puppy's early education. He was born without any bad habits. He does not know what is good or bad behavior. If he does things like

From puppyhood through adulthood, Portuguese Water Dogs crave interaction with their human families...just look at this excited trio awaiting their owner's return.

nipping and digging, it's because he is having fun and doesn't know that humans consider these things as "bad." It's your job to teach him proper puppy manners, and this is the best time to accomplish that…before he has developed bad habits, since it is much more difficult to "unlearn" or correct unacceptable learned behavior than to teach good behavior from the start.

Make sure that all members of the family understand the importance of being consistent when training their new puppy. If you tell the puppy to stay off the sofa and your daughter allows him to cuddle on the couch to watch her favorite television show, your pup will be confused about what he is and is not allowed to do. Have a family conference before your pup comes home so that everyone understands the basic principles of puppy training and the rules you have set forth for the pup, and agrees to follow them.

A polite Portuguese Water dog sits patiently while his collar and lead are put on. He knows who's the boss!

The old adage that "an ounce of prevention is worth a pound of cure" is especially true when it comes to puppies. It is much easier to prevent inappropriate behavior than it is to change it. It's also easier and less stressful for the pup, since it will keep discipline to a minimum and create a more positive learning environment for him. That, in turn, will also be easier on you.

Here are a few commonsense tips to keep your belongings safe and your puppy out of trouble:

MAKE A COMMITMENT

Dogs are most assuredly man's best friend, but they are also a lot of work. When you add a puppy to your family, you also are adding to your daily responsibilities for years to come. Dogs need more than just food, water and a place to sleep. They also require training (which can be ongoing throughout the lifetime of the dog), activity to keep them physically and mentally fit and hands-on attention every day, plus grooming and health care. Your life as you now know it may well disappear! Are you prepared for such drastic changes?

- Keep your closet doors closed and your shoes, socks and other apparel off the floor so your puppy can't get at them.
- Keep a secure lid on the trash container or put the trash where your puppy can't dig into it. He can't damage what he can't reach!
- Supervise your puppy at all times to make sure he is not getting into mischief. If he starts to chew the corner of the rug, you can distract him instantly by tossing a toy for him to fetch. You also will be able to whisk him outside when you notice that he is about to piddle on the carpet. If you can't see your puppy, you can't teach or correct his behavior.

Any young person will be happy to have PWD "siblings" as part of the family pack.

SOLVING PUPPY PROBLEMS

Chewing and Nipping

Nipping at fingers and toes is normal puppy behavior. Chewing is also the way that puppies investigate their surroundings. However, you will have to teach your puppy that chewing anything other than his toys is not acceptable. That won't happen overnight and at times puppy teeth will test your patience. However, if you allow nipping and chewing to continue, just think about the damage that a mature PWD can do with a full set of adult teeth.

Whenever your puppy nips your hand or fingers, cry out "Ouch!" in a loud voice, which should startle your puppy and stop him from nipping, even if only for a moment. Immediately distract him by offering a small treat or an appropriate toy for him to chew instead (which means having chew toys and puppy treats handy or in your pockets at all times). Praise him when he takes the toy and tell him what a good fellow he is. Praise is just as or even more important in puppy training as discipline and correction.

Puppies also tend to nip at children more often than adults, since they perceive little ones to be more vulnerable and more similar to their littermates. Teach your children appropriate responses to nipping behavior. If they are unable to handle it themselves, you may have to intervene. Puppy nips can be quite painful and a child's frightened reaction will only encourage a puppy to nip harder, which is a natural canine response. As with all other puppy situations, interaction between your PWD puppy and children should be supervised.

Chewing on objects, not just family members' fingers and ankles, is also normal canine behavior that can be especially tedious (for the owner, not the pup) during the teething period when the puppy's adult teeth are coming in. At this stage, chewing just plain feels good. Furniture legs and cabinet corners are common puppy favorites. Shoes and other personal items also taste pretty good to a pup.

The best solution is, once again, prevention. If you value something, keep it tucked away and out of reach. You can't hide your dining-room table in a closet, but you can try to deflect the chewing by applying a bitter product made just to deter dogs from chewing. Available in a

A PWD pup is a bright, alert and charming youngster just waiting to steal your heart!

A SMILE'S WORTH A MILE

Don't embark on your puppy's training course when you're not in the mood. Never train your puppy if you're feeling grouchy or impatient with him. Subjecting your puppy to your bad mood is a bad move. Your pup will sense your negative attitude, and neither of you will enjoy the session or have any measure of success. Always begin and end your training sessions on a happy note.

spray or cream, this substance is vile-tasting, although safe for dogs, and most puppies will avoid the forbidden object after one tiny taste. You also can apply the product to your leather leash if the puppy tries to chew on his lead during leash-training sessions.

Keep a ready supply of safe chews handy to offer your PWD as a distraction when he starts to chew on something that's a "no-no." Remember, at this tender age he does not yet know what is permitted or forbidden, so you have to be "on call" every minute he's awake and on the prowl.

There is simply no better way to train your puppy and provide for his safety than to use a suitable crate.

You may lose a treasure or two during puppy's growing-up period, and the furniture could sustain a nasty nick or two. These can be trying times, so be prepared for those inevitable accidents and comfort yourself in knowing that this too shall pass.

"Counter Surfing"

What we like to call "counter surfing" is a normal activity for many dogs and usually starts to happen as soon as a puppy realizes that he is big enough to stand on his hind legs and investigate the good stuff on the kitchen counter or the coffee table. Once again, you have to be there to prevent it! As soon as you see your PWD even start to raise himself up, startle him with a sharp "No!" or "Aaahh, aaahh!" If he succeeds and manages to get one or both paws on the forbidden surface, smack those paws (firmly but gently) and tell him "Off!" As soon as he's back on all four paws, command him to sit and praise at once.

For surf prevention, make sure to keep any tempting treats or edibles out of reach, where your PWD can't see or smell them. It's the old rule of prevention yet again.

Domestic Squabbles

How well your new PWD will get along with an older dog who has squatter's rights depends largely on the individual dogs. Like people, some dogs are more gregarious than others and will enjoy having a furry friend to play with. Others will not be thrilled at the prospect of sharing their dog space with another canine. Fortunately, the PWD is a friendly creature who gets along with other animals, but will any pets already in the household be happy to welcome the new addition?

It's best to introduce the dogs to each other on neutral ground, away from home, so the resident dog won't feel so possessive. Keep both puppy and adult on loose leads (loose is very important, as a tight lead sends negative signals and can intimidate either dog) and allow them to sniff and do their doggy things. A few raised hackles are normal, with the older dog pawing at the youngster. Let the two work things out between them unless you see signs of real aggression, such as deep growls or curled lips and serious snarls. You may have to keep them separated until the veteran gets used to the new family member, often after the pup has outgrown the silly puppy stage and is more mature in stature. Take precautions to make sure that the puppy does not become frightened by the older dog's behavior.

Whatever happens, it's important to make your resident dog feel secure. (Jealousy is normal among dogs, too!) Pay extra attention to the older dog: feed him first, hug him first and don't insist he share his toys or space with the new pup until he's ready. If the two are still at odds months later, consult an obedience professional for advice.

Cat introductions are easier, believe it or not. Being agile and independent creatures, cats will scoot to high places, out of the puppy's reach. A cat might even tease the puppy and cuff him from above when the pup comes within paw's reach. However, most will end up buddies if you just let dog-and-cat nature run its course.

THE FAMILY FELINE

A resident cat has feline squatter's rights. The cat will treat the newcomer (your puppy) as she sees fit, regardless of what you do or say. So it's best to let the two of them work things out on their own terms. Cats have a height advantage and will generally leap to higher ground to avoid direct contact with a rambunctious pup. Some will hiss and boldly swat at a pup who passes by or tries to reach the cat. Keep the puppy under control in the presence of the cat and they will eventually become accustomed to each other.

Here's a hint: move the cat's litter box where the puppy can't get into it! It's best to do so well before the pup comes home so the cat is used to the new location.

PROPER CARE OF YOUR PORTUGUESE WATER DOG

Adding a PWD to your household means adding a new family member who will need your care each and every day. When your PWD pup first comes home, you will start a routine with him so that, as he grows up, your dog will have a daily schedule just as you do. The aspects of your dog's daily care will likewise become regular parts of your day, so you'll both have a new schedule. Dogs learn by consistency and thrive on routine: regular times for meals, exercise, grooming and potty trips are just as important for your dog as they are to you! Your dog's schedule will depend much on your family's daily routine, but remember that you now have a new member of the family who is part of your day every day.

FEEDING

Feeding your dog the best diet is based on various factors, including age, activity level, overall condition and size of breed. When you visit the breeder, he will share with you his advice about the proper diet for your dog based on his experience with the breed and the foods with which he has had success. Likewise, your vet will be a helpful source of advice throughout the dog's life and will aid you in planning a diet for optimal health.

FEEDING THE PUPPY

Of course, your pup's very first food will be his dam's milk. There may be special situations in which pups fail to nurse, necessitating that the breeder hand-feed them with a formula, but, for the most part, pups spend the first weeks of life nursing from their dam. The breeder weans the pups by gradually introducing solid foods and decreasing the milk meals. Pups may even start themselves off on the weaning process, albeit inadvertently, if they snatch bites from their mom's food bowl.

By the time the pups are ready for new homes, they are fully weaned and eating a good puppy food. As a new owner, you may be thinking, "Great! The breeder has taken care of the hard part." Not so fast.

A puppy's first year of life is the time when all or most of his growth and development takes place. This is a delicate time, and diet plays a huge role in proper skeletal and muscular formation. Improper diet and exercise habits can lead to damaging problems that will compromise the dog's health and movement for his entire life. The focus should be on healthy, stable growth, not rapid growth. That being said, new owners should not worry needlessly. With the myriad types of food formulated specifically for growing pups of different-sized breeds, dog-food manufacturers have taken much of the guesswork out of feeding your puppy well. Since growth-food formulas are designed to provide the nutrition that a growing puppy needs, it is unnecessary and, in fact, can prove harmful to add supplements to the diet. Research has shown that too much of certain vitamin supplements and minerals predispose a dog to skeletal problems. It's by no means a case of "if a little is good, a lot is better." At every stage of your dog's life, too much or too little in the way of nutrients can be harmful, which is why a manufactured complete food is the easiest way to know that your dog is getting what he needs.

Because of a young pup's small body and accordingly small digestive system, his daily portion will be divided up into

Initially, your new puppy should be offered the same food to which he became accustomed when under the breeder's care. Any dietary changes should be made gradually.

NOT HUNGRY?

No dog in his right mind would turn down his dinner, would he? If you notice that your dog has lost interest in his food, there could be any number of causes. Dental problems are a common cause of appetite loss, one that is often overlooked. If your dog has a toothache, a loose tooth or sore gums from infection, chances are it doesn't feel so good to chew. Think about when you've had a toothache! If your dog does not approach the food bowl with his usual enthusiasm, look inside his mouth for signs of a problem. Whatever the cause, you'll want to consult your vet so that your chow hound can get back to his happy, hungry self as soon as possible.

small meals throughout the day. This can mean starting off with three or more meals a day and decreasing the number of meals as the pup matures. It is generally thought that, for the adult dog, dividing the day's food into two meals on a morning/evening schedule is healthiest for the dog's digestion.

Regarding the feeding schedule, feeding the pup at the same times and in the same place each day is important for both housebreaking purposes and establishing the dog's everyday routine. As for the amount to feed, growing puppies generally need proportionately more food per body weight than their adult counterparts, but a pup should never be allowed to gain excess weight. Dogs of all ages should be kept in proper body condition, but extra weight can strain a pup's developing frame, causing skeletal problems.

Watch your pup's weight as he grows and, if the recommended amounts seem to be too much or too little for your pup, consult the vet about appropriate dietary changes. Keep in mind that treats, although small, can quickly add up throughout the day, contributing unnecessary calories. Treats are fine when used prudently; opt for dog treats specially formulated to be healthy or for nutritious snacks like small pieces of cheese or cooked chicken.

FEEDING THE ADULT DOG

For the adult (meaning physically mature) dog, feeding properly is about maintenance, not growth. Again, correct weight is a concern. Your dog should appear fit and should have an evident "waist." His ribs should not be protruding (a sign of being underweight), but they should be covered by only a slight layer of fat. Under normal circumstances, an adult dog can be maintained fairly easily with a high-quality nutritionally complete adult-formula food.

Factor treats into your dog's overall daily caloric intake, and avoid offering table scraps. Certain "people foods," including chocolate, raisins, grapes, nuts and onions, are toxic to dogs; further, feeding from the table encourages begging and overeating. Overweight dogs are more prone to health problems. Research has even shown that obesity takes years off a dog's life. With that in mind, resist the urge to overfeed and over-treat. Don't make unnecessary additions to your dog's diet, whether with tidbits or with extra vitamins and minerals.

The amount of food needed for proper maintenance will vary depending on the individual dog's activity level, but you will be able to tell whether the daily portions are keeping him in good shape. With the wide variety of good complete foods available, choosing what to feed is largely a matter of personal preference. Just as with the puppy, the adult dog should have consistency in his

For the puppy, feeding and house-training go hand in hand—what goes in must come out!

SWITCHING FOODS

There are certain times in a dog's life when it becomes necessary to switch his food; for example, from puppy to adult food and then from adult to senior-dog food. Additionally, you may decide to feed your pup a different type of food from what he received from the breeder, and there may be "emergency" situations in which you can't find your dog's normal brand and have to offer something else temporarily. Anytime a change is made, for whatever reason, the switch must be done gradually. You don't want to upset the dog's stomach or end up with a picky eater who refuses to eat something new. A tried-and-true approach is, over the course of about a week, to mix a little of the new food in with the old, increasing the proportion of new to old as the days progress. At the end of the week, you'll be feeding his regular portions of the new food, and he will barely notice the change.

mealtimes and feeding place. In addition to a consistent routine, regular mealtimes also allow the owner to see how much his dog is eating. If the dog seems never to be satisfied or, likewise, becomes uninterested in his food, the owner will know right away that something is wrong and can consult the vet.

DIET DON'TS

- Got milk? Don't give it to your dog! Dogs cannot tolerate large quantities of cows' milk, as they do not have the enzymes to digest lactose.
- You may have heard of dog owners who add raw eggs to their dogs' food for a shiny coat or to make the food more palatable, but consumption of raw eggs too often can cause a deficiency of the vitamin biotin.
- Avoid feeding table scraps, as they will upset the balance of the dog's complete food. Additionally, fatty or highly seasoned foods can cause upset canine stomachs.
- Do not offer raw meat to your dog. Raw meat can contain parasites; it also is high in fat.
- Vitamin A toxicity in dogs can be caused by too much raw liver, especially if the dog already gets enough vitamin A in his balanced diet, which should be the case.
- Bones like chicken, pork chop and other soft bones are not suitable, as they easily splinter.

Diets for the Aging Dog

A good rule of thumb is that once a dog has reached 75% of his expected lifespan, he has reached "senior citizen" or geriatric status. Your PWD will be considered a senior at about 8 years of age; he has a projected lifespan of about 10–15 years, 12 being the average. (The smallest breeds generally enjoy the longest lives and the largest breeds the shortest.)

What does aging have to do with your dog's diet? No, he won't get a discount at the local diner's early-bird special. Yes, he will require some dietary changes to accommodate the changes that come along with increased age. One change is that the older dog's dietary needs become more similar to that of a puppy. Specifically, dogs can metabolize more protein as youngsters and seniors than in the adult-maintenance stage. Discuss with your vet whether you need to switch to a higher-protein or senior-formulated food or whether your current adult-dog food contains sufficient nutrition for the senior.

Watching the dog's weight remains essential, even more so in the senior stage. Older dogs are already more vulnerable to illness, and obesity only contributes to their susceptibility to problems. As the older dog becomes less active and, thus, exercises less, his regular portions may cause him to gain weight. At this point, you may consider decreasing his daily food intake or switching to a reduced-calorie food. As with other changes, you should consult your vet for advice.

DON'T FORGET THE WATER!

For a dog, it's always time for a drink! Regardless of what type of food he eats, there's no doubt that he needs plenty of water. Fresh cold water, in a clean bowl, should be freely available to your dog at all times. There are special circumstances, such as during puppy housebreaking, when you will want to monitor your pup's water intake so that you will be able to predict when he will need to relieve himself, but water must be available to him nonetheless. Water is essential for hydration and proper body function just as it is in humans.

You will get to know how much your dog typically drinks in a day. Of course, in the heat or if exercising vigorously, he will be more thirsty and will drink more. However, if he begins to drink noticeably more water for no apparent reason, this could signal any of various problems, and you are advised to consult your vet.

Water is the best drink for dogs. Some owners are tempted to give milk from time to time or to moisten dry food with milk, but dogs do not have the enzymes necessary to digest the lactose in milk, which is much different from the milk that nursing puppies receive. Therefore, stick with clean fresh water to quench your dog's thirst, and always have it readily available to him.

PWDs of all ages need a supply of water available to them so that they can quench their thirst whenever they need to.

EXERCISE

We all know the importance of exercise for humans, so it should come as no surprise that it is essential for our canine friends as well. Now, regardless of your own level of fitness, get ready to assume the role of personal trainer for your dog. It's not as hard as it sounds, and it will have health benefits for you, too.

Just as with anything else you do with your dog, you must set a routine for his exercise. It's the same as your daily morning run

PUPPY STEPS

Puppies are brimming with activity and enthusiasm. It seems that they can play all day and night without tiring, but don't overdo your puppy's exercise regimen. Easy does it for the puppy's first six to nine months. Keep walks brief and don't let the puppy engage in stressful jumping games. The puppy frame is delicate, and too much exercise during those critical growing months can cause injury to his bone structure, ligaments and musculature. Save his first jog for his first birthday!

before work or never missing the 7 p.m. aerobics class. If you plan it and get into the habit of actually doing it, it will become just another part of your day. Think of it as making daily exercise appointments with your dog, and stick to your schedule.

As a rule, dogs in normal health should have half an hour of activity each day at the very least. Dogs with health or orthopedic problems may have specific limitations, so their exercise plans are best devised with the help of a vet. For healthy dogs, there are many ways to fit 30 minutes of activity into your day and your PWD will certainly welcome the opportunity for more than a half-hour's worth of activity. Depending on your schedule, you may plan a 15-minute walk or activity session in the morning and again in the evening, or do it all at once in a half-hour session each day. Walking is the most popular way to exercise a dog (it's good for you, too!); other suggestions include retrieving games, jogging and disc-catching or other active games with his toys. If you have a safe body of water nearby, swimming is of course the most natural form of exercise for the PWD, putting no stress on his frame and thoroughly enjoyed. After all, "water" is his middle name!

For overweight dogs, dietary changes and activity will help the goal of weight loss. (Sound familiar?) While they should of course be encouraged to be active, remember not to overdo it, as the excess weight is already putting strain on his vital organs and bones. As for highly active dogs, some of them never seem to tire! They will enjoy time spent with their owners doing things together.

Regardless of your dog's condition and activity level, exercise offers benefits to all dogs and owners. Consider the fact that dogs who are kept active are more stimulated both physically and mentally, meaning that they are less likely to become bored and lapse into destructive behavior. Also consider the benefits of one-on-one time with your dog every day, continually strengthening the bond between the two of you. Furthermore, exercising together will improve health and longevity for both of you. You both need exercise, and now you and your dog have a workout partner and motivator!

GROOMING

A welcome miracle for people with dog allergies, the Portuguese Water Dog has a low-shedding coat with no undercoat. There are two acceptable coat types: curly, in which the hair is short and dense, lying close to the body in compact curls; and wavy, in which the hair is fairly long and lies in loose waves. Both coats require regular brushing to stay healthy and tangle-free.

The clip in which you keep your PWD is up to you; there are two clips for the breed: the lion clip, which is the traditional clip, and the retriever clip. Both clips are seen on show dogs in the US. A helpful illustrated grooming guide for both clips and both coat types can be found on the PWDCA's website at www.pwdca.org.

In the retriever clip, which is easier to trim and maintain, especially for pets, the entire coat is scissored or clipped to a uniform length of one inch all over the body. The only exception is the end of the tail, which is kept long. The lion clip is more elaborate and requires more skill and practice to execute correctly. The dog's hindquarters are clipped short, starting from about the halfway point of the dog's back, and the muzzle is clipped short as well. The front of the coat (head, neck, chest and forequarters) is kept long to resemble a lion's mane; the end of the tail is kept long as well.

Since the coat is hair and not fur, it will continue to grow and will still require regular trimming and brushing in either clip. Whether your dog is curly- or wavy-coated, be prepared to brush your PWD every couple of days to control knots and mats and to keep your dog looking magnificent. Although the coat does not shed or molt as do dogs with double coats, it requires brushing and combing to prevent tangling, to maintain healthy skin and haircoat and to remove

IMPROPER COATS

Sometimes a PWD pup is born with what is known as an "improper coat." While this is purely a cosmetic fault and affected puppies are still as healthy, intelligent and strong as properly coated PWDs, this type of coat is unacceptable in the show ring.

An improper coat is shorter and smoother, with tufts and with feathering on the backs of the legs. Sometimes improperly coated PWDs have double coats, and there is some evidence suggesting that they shed more than their properly coated counterparts and, thus, are not good choices for people with allergies.

A solid, non-slip grooming table should be used.

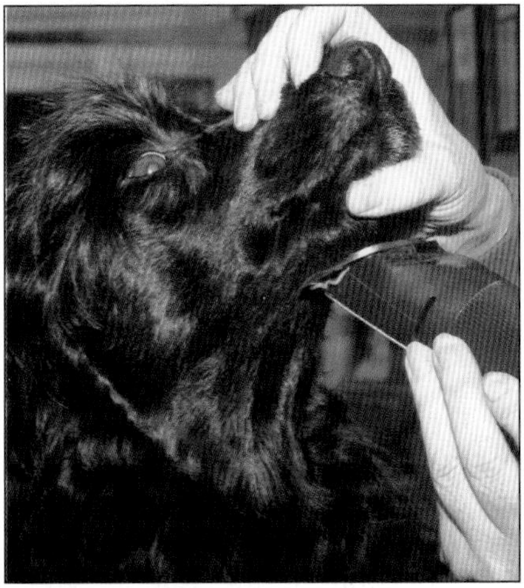

In the lion clip, the muzzle is trimmed short. Here electric clippers get the job done.

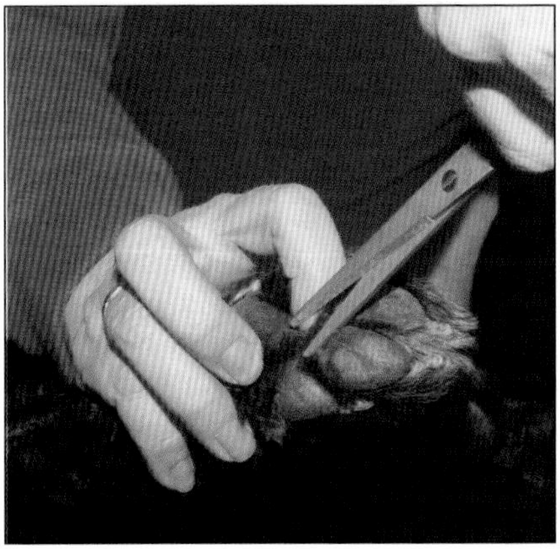

Regardless of which clip you choose, the hair between the footpads should always be trimmed. This "cleans up" the foot and removes excess hair, which can cause irritation.

broken hairs, shed hairs caught in the coat and accumulated debris.

BATHING

In general, dogs need to be bathed only a few times a year, possibly more often if your dog gets into something messy or if he starts to smell like a dog. Show dogs are usually bathed before every show, which could be as frequent as weekly, although this depends on the owner. Bathing too frequently can have negative effects on the skin and coat, removing natural oils and causing dryness. Also consider that a PWD who swims frequently will be getting regular baths the natural way.

If you give your dog his first bath when he is young, he will become accustomed to the process. Wrestling a dog into the tub or chasing a freshly shampooed dog who has escaped from the bath will be no fun! Most dogs don't naturally enjoy their baths, but you at least want yours to cooperate with you.

Before bathing the dog, have the items you'll need close at hand. First, decide where you will bathe the dog. You should have a tub or basin with a non-slip surface. Puppies can even be bathed in a sink. In warm weather, some like to use a portable pool in the yard, although you'll want to make sure your dog doesn't head for the nearest dirt pile following his bath! You will also need a hose or shower spray to wet the coat thoroughly, a shampoo formulated for dogs, absorbent towels and perhaps a blow dryer. Human shampoos are too harsh for dogs' coats and will dry them out.

Before wetting the dog, give him a brush-through to remove any dead hair, dirt and mats. Make sure he is at ease in the tub and have the water at a comfortable temperature. Begin bathing by wetting the coat all the way down to the skin. Massage in the shampoo, keeping it away from his face and eyes. Rinse him thoroughly, again avoiding the eyes and ears, as you don't want to get water into the ear canals. A thorough rinsing is important, as shampoo residue is drying and itchy to the dog. After rinsing, wrap him in a towel to absorb the initial moisture. You can finish drying with either a towel or a blow dryer on low heat, held at a safe distance from the dog. You should keep the dog indoors and away from drafts until he is completely dry.

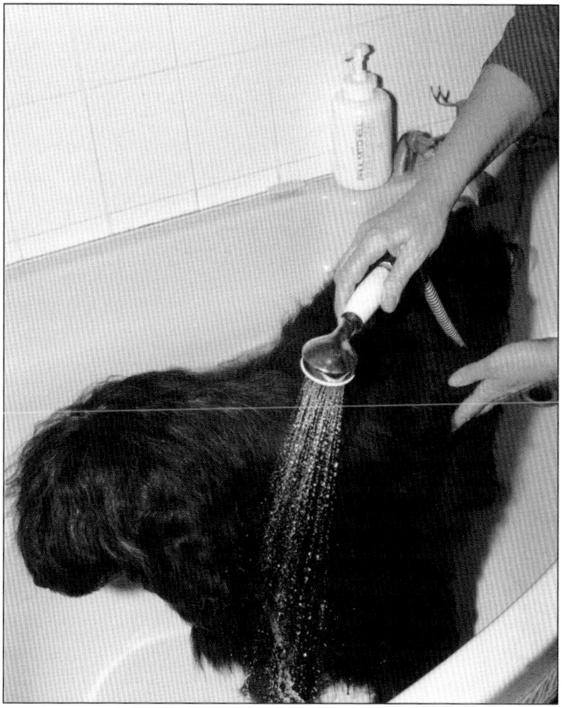

The dog's coat should be thoroughly wet before the shampoo is applied. Only use shampoo made for use on dogs.

Nail Clipping

Having his nails trimmed is not on many dogs' lists of favorite things to do. With this in mind, you will need to accustom your puppy to the procedure at a young age so that he will sit still (well, as still as he can) for his pedicures. Long nails can cause the dog's feet to spread, which is not good for him; likewise, long nails can hurt if they unintentionally scratch, not good for you!

Some dogs' nails are worn down naturally by regular walking on hard surfaces, so the frequency with which you clip depends on your individual dog. Look at his nails from time to time and clip as needed; a good way to know when it's time for a trim is if you hear your dog clicking as he walks across the floor.

There are several types of nail clippers and even nail-grinding tools made for dogs; first we'll

In the lion clip, the hair is trimmed short, working backwards from about the middle of the body.

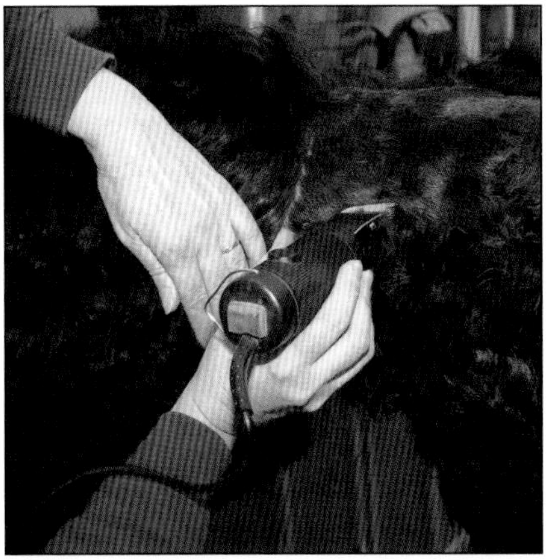

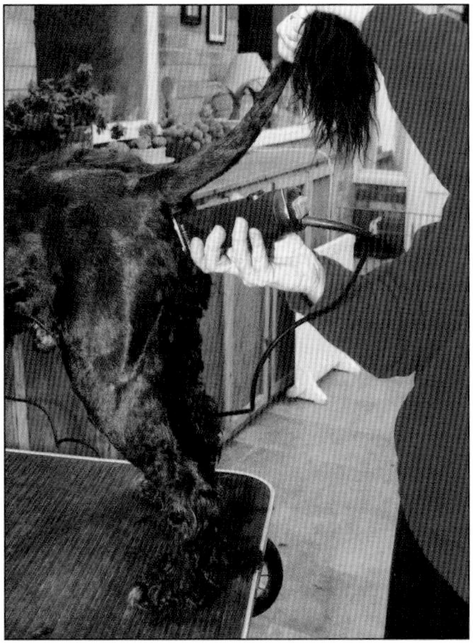

Take care when grooming the sensitive areas, such as the base of the tail.

The base of the tail is clipped short, leaving the end long.

Before and after—the left side is trimmed, the right side is not.

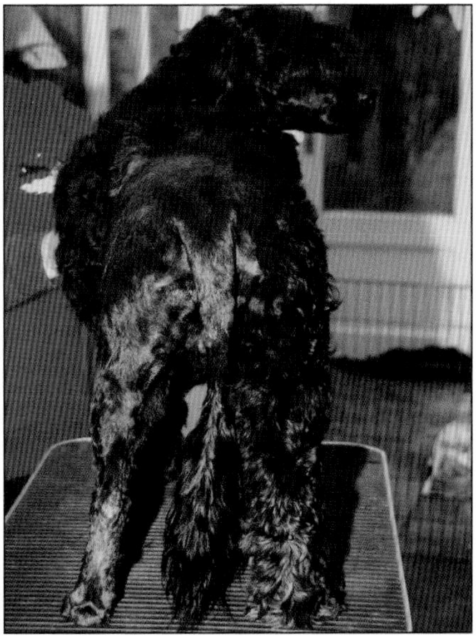

A side view of the finished lion clip.

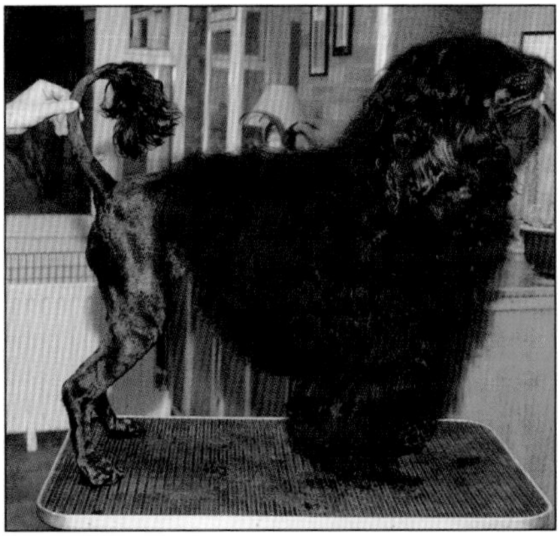

discuss using the clipper. To start, have your clipper ready and some doggie treats on hand. You want your pup to view his nail-clipping sessions in a positive light, and what better way to convince him than with food? You may want to enlist the help of an assistant to comfort the pup and offer treats as you concentrate on the clipping itself. The guillotine-type clipper is thought of by many as the easiest type to use; the nail tip is inserted into the opening, and blades on the top and bottom snip it off in one clip.

Start by grasping the pup's paw; a little pressure on the foot pad causes the nail to extend, making it easier to clip. Clip off a little at a time. If you can see the "quick," which is a blood vessel that runs through each nail, you will know how much to trim, as you do not want to cut into the quick. On that note, if you do cut the quick, which will cause bleeding, you can stem the flow of blood with a styptic pencil or other clotting agent. If you mistakenly nip the quick, do not panic or fuss, as this will cause the pup to be afraid. Simply reassure the pup, stop the bleeding and move on to the next nail. Don't be discouraged; you will become a professional canine pedicurist with practice.

You may or may not be able to see the quick, so it's best to

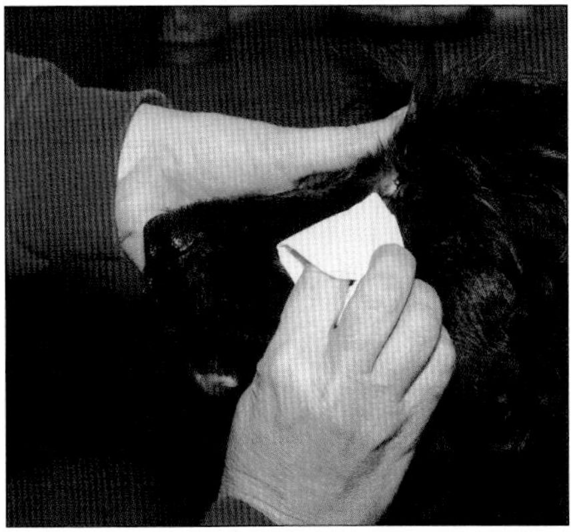

The area around your PWD's eyes can be cleaned with a soft wipe.

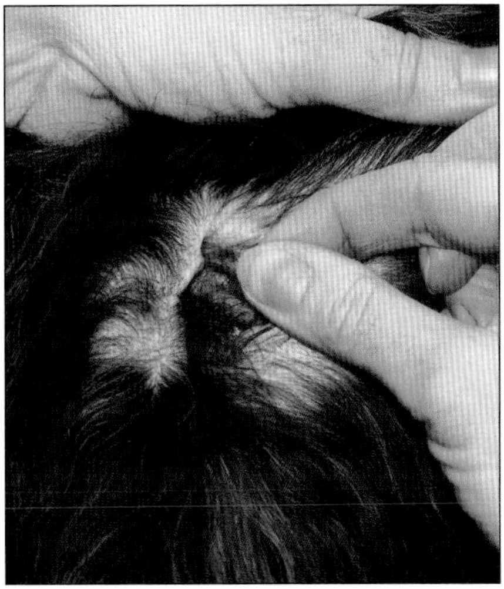

Using your fingers, the excess long hairs can be plucked from the dog's ears.

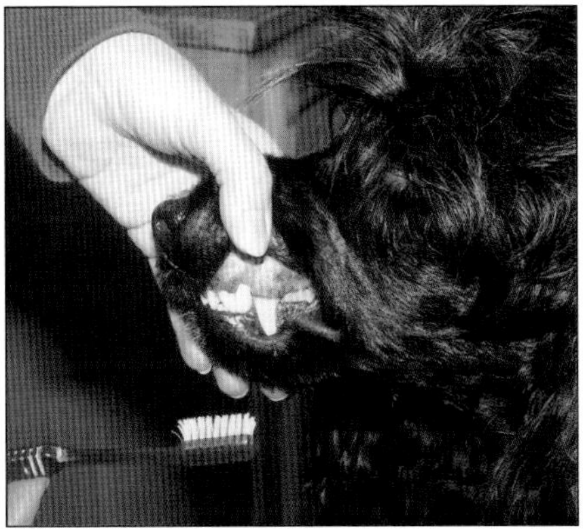

Brush your PWD's teeth with a toothbrush and toothpaste that are specially made for dogs.

just clip off a small bit at a time. If you see a dark dot in the center of the nail, this is the quick and your cue to stop clipping. Tell the puppy he's a "good boy" and offer a piece of treat with each nail. You can also use nail-clipping time to examine the footpads, making sure that they are not dry and cracked and that nothing has become embedded in them.

The nail grinder, the other choice, is many owners' first choice. Accustoming the puppy to the sound of the grinder and sensation of the buzz presents fewer challenges than the clipper, and there's no chance of cutting through the quick. Use the grinder on a low setting and always talk soothingly to your dog. He won't mind his salon visit, and he'll have nicely polished nails as well.

Your local pet shop will have nail clippers made especially for dogs' tough nails.

Ear Cleaning

While keeping your dog's ears clean unfortunately will not cause him to "hear" your commands any better, it will protect him from ear infection and ear-mite infestation. In addition, a dog's ears are vulnerable to waxy build-up and to collecting foreign matter from the outdoors. Look in your dog's ears regularly to ensure that they look pink, clean and otherwise healthy. Even if they look fine, an odor in the ears signals a problem and means it's time to call the vet.

A dog's ears should be cleaned regularly; once a week is suggested, and you can do this along with your regular brushing. Using a cotton ball or pad and never probing into the ear canal, wipe the ear gently. You can use an ear-cleansing liquid or powder available from your vet or pet-supply store; alternatively, you might prefer to use home-made solutions with ingredients like one part white vinegar and one part hydrogen peroxide. Ask your vet about home remedies before you attempt to concoct something on your own!

Keep your dog's ears free of excess hair by plucking it as

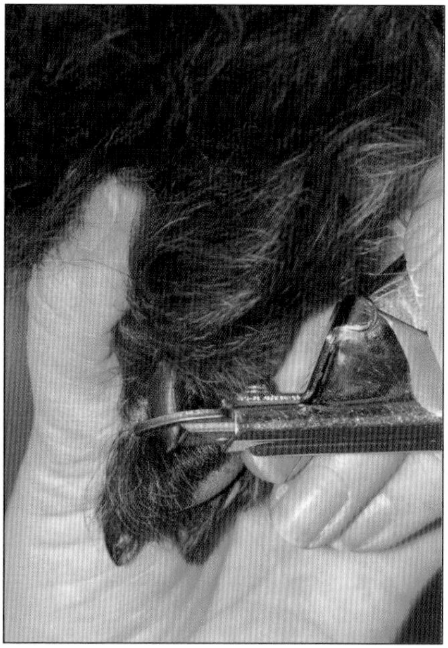

SCOOTING HIS BOTTOM

Here's a doggy problem that many owners tend to neglect. If your dog is scooting his rear end around the carpet, he probably is experiencing anal-sac impaction or blockage. The anal sacs are the two grape-sized glands on either side of the dog's vent. The dog cannot empty these glands, which become filled with a foul-smelling material. The dog may attempt to lick the area to relieve the pressure. He may also rub his anus on your walls, furniture or floors.

Don't neglect your dog's rear end during grooming sessions. By squeezing both sides of the anus with a soft cloth, you can express some of the material in the sacs. If the material is pasty and thick, you likely will need the assistance of a veterinarian. Vets know how to express the glands and can show you how to do it correctly without hurting the dog or spraying yourself with the foul liquid.

A dog that is exercised regularly on pavement will not experience discomfort from over-grown nails, as the hard surface will wear down the nails.

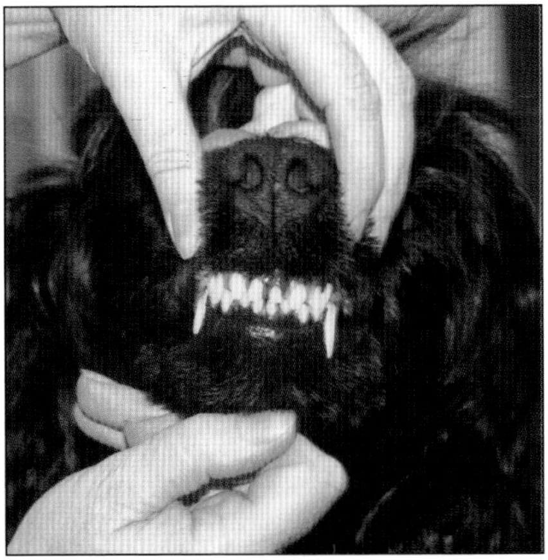

Check your PWD's mouth regularly to make sure that his teeth and gums are healthy.

needed. If done gently, this will be painless for the dog. Look for wax, brown droppings (a sign of ear mites), redness or any other abnormalities. At the first sign of a problem, contact your vet so that he can prescribe an appropriate medication.

EYE CARE

During grooming sessions, pay extra attention to the condition of your dog's eyes. If the area around the eyes is soiled or if tear staining has occurred, there are various cleaning agents made especially for this purpose. Look at the dog's eyes to make sure no debris has entered; dogs with large eyes and those who spend time outdoors are especially prone to this.

The signs of an eye infection are obvious: mucus, redness, puffiness, scabs or other signs of irritation. If your dog's eyes become infected, the vet will likely prescribe an antibiotic ointment for treatment. If you notice signs of more serious problems, such as opacities in the eye, which usually indicate cataracts, consult the vet at once. Taking time to pay attention to your dog's eyes will alert you in the early stages of any problem so that you can get your dog treatment as soon as possible. You could save your dog's sight!

IDENTIFICATION AND TRAVEL

ID for Your Dog

You love your PWD and want to keep him safe. Of course, you take every precaution to prevent his escaping from the yard or becoming lost or stolen. You have a sturdy high fence and you always keep your dog on lead when out and about in public places. If your dog is not properly identified, however, you are overlooking a major aspect of his safety. We hope to never be in a

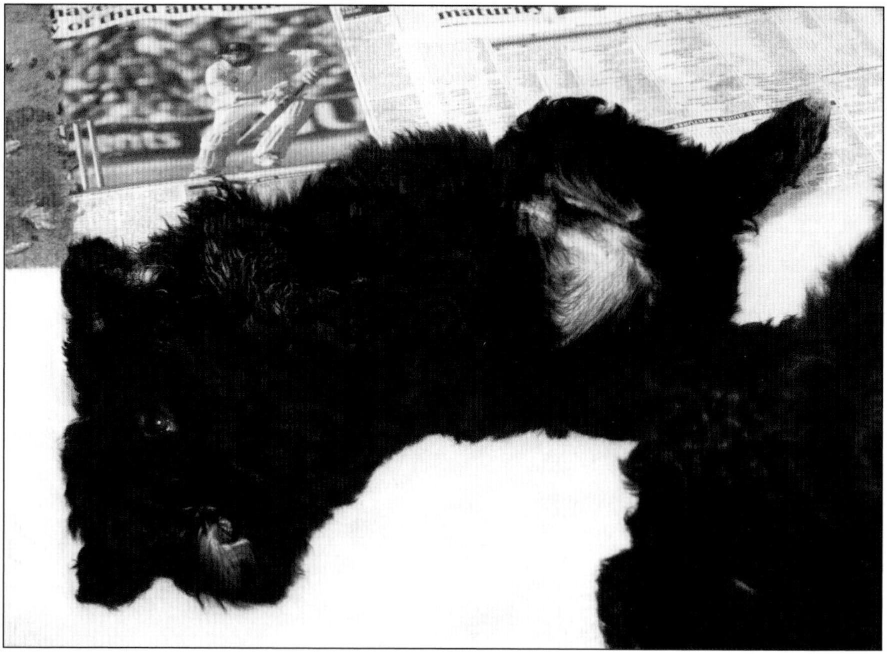

Tattooing is a permanent form of identification for your dog that can be done by your vet. The pink skin on the belly or the inside of the ear are usual locations for the tattoo so that it is easily visible.

PET OR STRAY?

Besides the obvious benefit of providing your contact information to whoever finds your lost dog, an ID tag makes your dog more approachable and more likely to be recovered. A strange dog wandering the neighborhood without a collar and tags will look like a stray, while the collar and tags indicate that the dog is someone's pet. Even if the ID tags become detached from the collar, the collar alone will make a person more likely to pick up the dog.

situation where our dog is missing, but we should practice prevention in the unfortunate case that this happens; identification greatly increases the chances of your dog's being returned to you.

There are several ways to identify your dog. First, the traditional dog tag should be a staple in your dog's wardrobe, attached to his everyday collar. Tags can be made of sturdy plastic and various metals and should include your contact information so that a person who finds the dog can get in touch with you right away to arrange his return. Many people today enjoy the wide range of decorative tags available, so have fun and create a tag to match your dog's personality. Of course, it is important that the tag stays on the collar, so have a secure "O" ring attachment; you also can explore the type of tag that slides right onto the collar.

In addition to the ID tag, which every dog should wear even if identified by another method, two other forms of identification have become popular: microchipping and tattooing. In microchipping, a tiny scannable chip is painlessly inserted under the dog's skin. The number is registered to you so that, if your lost dog turns up at a clinic or shelter, the chip can be scanned to retrieve your contact information.

The advantage of the microchip is that it is a permanent form of ID, but there are

PWDs love time outdoors. Part of grooming means checking the coat after outings to rid the coat of dirt and debris and to check for fleas, ticks, insect bites, allergens or other irritants.

some factors to consider. Several different companies make microchips, and not all are compatible with the others' scanning devices. It's best to find a company with a universal microchip that can be read by scanners made by other companies as well. It won't do any good to have the dog chipped if the information cannot be retrieved. Also, not every humane society, shelter and clinic is equipped with a scanner, although more and more facilities are equipping themselves. In fact, many shelters microchip dogs that they adopt out to new homes.

Because the microchip is not visible to the eye, the dog must wear a tag that states that he is microchipped so that whoever picks him up will know to have him scanned. He of course also should have a tag with contact information in case his chip cannot be read. Humane societies and veterinary clinics offer microchipping service, which is usually very affordable.

Though less popular than microchipping, tattooing is another permanent method of ID for dogs. Most vets perform this service, and there are also clinics that perform dog tattooing. This is also an affordable procedure and one that will not cause much discomfort for the dog. It is best to put the tattoo in a visible area, such as the ear, to deter theft. It is sad to say that there are cases of dogs' being stolen and sold to research laboratories, but such laboratories will not accept tattooed dogs.

To ensure that the tattoo is effective in aiding your dog's return to you, the tattoo number must be registered with a national organization. That way,

YOUR PACK ANIMAL

If you are bringing your dog along with you on a vacation, here's a list of the things you want to pack for him:

- leashes (conventional and retractable)
- collar with ID tag
- dog food and bottled water
- grooming tools
- flea and tick sprays
- crate and crate pad
- pooper-scooper and plastic bags
- toys and treats
- towels and paper towels
- first-aid kit
- dog license and rabies certificate

when someone finds a tattooed dog, a phone call to the registry will quickly match the dog with his owner.

Hit the Road

Car travel with your PWD may be limited to necessity only, such as trips to the vet, or you may bring your dog along almost everywhere you go. This will depend much on your individual dog and how he reacts to rides in the car. You can begin desensitizing your dog to car travel as a pup so that it's something that he's used to. Still, some dogs suffer from motion sickness. Your vet may prescribe a medication for this if trips in the car pose a problem for your dog. At the very least, you will need to get him to the vet, so he will need to tolerate these trips with the least amount of hassle possible.

Start taking your pup on short trips, maybe just around the block to start. If he is fine with short trips, lengthen your rides a little at a time. Start to take him on your errands or just for drives around town. By this time, it will be easy to tell whether your dog is a born traveler or would prefer staying at home when you are on the road.

Of course, safety is a concern for dogs in the car. First, he must travel securely, not left loose to roam about the car where he could be injured or distract the driver. A young pup can be held by a passenger initially but should soon graduate to a travel crate, which can be the same crate he uses in the home. Other options include a car harness (like a seat belt for dogs) and partitioning the back of the car with a gate made for this purpose.

Bring along what you will need for the dog. He should wear his collar and ID tags, of course, and you should bring his leash, water (and food if a long trip) and clean-up materials for potty breaks and in case of motion sickness. Always keep your dog on his leash when you make stops, and never leave him alone in the car. Many a dog has died from the heat inside a closed car; this does not take much time at all in any kind of weather. A dog left alone inside a car can also be a target for thieves.

FEEDING IN HOT WEATHER

Even the most dedicated chow hound may have less of an appetite when the weather is hot or humid. If your dog leaves more of his food behind than usual, adjust his portions until the weather and his appetite return to normal. Never leave the uneaten portion in the bowl, hoping he will return to finish it, because higher temperatures encourage food spoilage and bacterial growth.

TRAINING YOUR
PORTUGUESE WATER DOG

BASIC TRAINING PRINCIPLES: PUPPY VS. ADULT

There's a big difference between training an adult dog and training a young puppy. With a young puppy, everything is new. At eight to ten weeks of age, he will be experiencing many things, and he has nothing with which to compare these experiences. Up to this point, he has been with his dam and littermates, not one-on-one with people except in his interactions with his breeder and visitors to the litter.

When you first bring the puppy home, he is eager to please you. This means that he accepts doing things your way. During the next couple of months, he will absorb the basis of everything he needs to know for the rest of his life. This early age is even referred to as the "sponge" stage. After that, for the next 18 months, it's up to you to reinforce good manners by building on the foundation that you've established. Once your puppy is reliable in basic commands and behavior and has reached the appropriate age, you may gradually introduce him to some of the interesting sports, games and activities available to dog owners and their dogs.

Raising your puppy is a family affair. Each member of the family

LEADER OF THE PACK

Canines are pack animals. They live according to pack rules, and every pack has only one leader. Guess what? That's you! To establish your position of authority, lay down the rules and be fair and good-natured in all your dealings with your dog. He will consider young children as his littermates, but the one who trains him, who feeds him, who grooms him, who expects him to come into line, that's his leader. And he who leads must be obeyed.

must know what rules to set forth for the puppy and how to use the same one-word commands to mean exactly the same thing every time. Even if yours is a large family, one person will soon be considered by the pup to be the leader, the Alpha person in his pack, the "boss" who must be obeyed. Often that highly regarded person turns out to be the one who feeds the puppy. Food ranks very high on the puppy's list of important things! That's why your puppy is rewarded with small treats along with verbal praise when he responds to you correctly. As the puppy learns to do what you want him to do, the food rewards are gradually eliminated and only the praise remains. If you were to keep up with the food treats, you could have two problems on your hands—an obese dog and a beggar.

Here's where the bond begins...a PWD puppy leaves the breeder with his new owner to become part of a new home.

Training begins the minute your PWD puppy steps through the doorway of your home, so don't make the mistake of putting the puppy on the floor and telling him by your actions to "Go for it! Run wild!" Even if this is your first puppy, you must act as if you know what you're doing. Be the boss. An uncertain pup may be

WHO'S TRAINING WHOM?

Dog training is a black-and-white exercise. The correct response to a command must be absolute, and the trainer must insist on completely accurate responses from the dog. A trainer cannot command his dog to sit and then settle for the dog's melting into the down position. Often owners are so pleased that their dogs "did something" in response to a command that they just shrug and say, "OK, Down" even though they wanted the dog to sit. You want your dog to respond to the command without hesitation: he must respond at that moment and correctly every time.

terrified to move, while a bold one will be ready to take you at your word and start plotting to destroy the house! Before you collected your puppy, you decided where his own special place would be, and that's where to put him when you first arrive home. Give him a house tour after he has investigated his area and had a nap and a bathroom "pit stop."

Every puppy wants to dive headfirst into dinner, but good manners around food must be instilled in the pup at an early age.

SMILE WHEN YOU ORDER ME AROUND!

While trainers recommend practicing with your dog every day, it's perfectly acceptable to take a "mental health day" off. It's better not to train the dog on days when you're in a sour mood. Your bad attitude or lack of interest will be sensed by your dog, and he will respond accordingly. Studies show that dogs are well tuned in to their humans' emotions. Be conscious of how you use your voice when talking to your dog. Raising your voice or shouting will only erode your dog's trust in you as his trainer and master.

It's worth mentioning here that, if you've adopted an adult dog that is completely trained to your liking, lucky you! You're off the hook! However, if that dog spent his life up to this point in a kennel, or even in a good home but without any real training, be prepared to tackle the job ahead. A dog three years of age or older with no previous training cannot be blamed for not knowing what he was never taught. While the dog is trying to understand and learn your rules, at the same time he has to unlearn many of his previously self-taught habits and general view of the world.

Working with a professional trainer will speed up your progress with an adopted adult dog. You'll need patience, too. Some new rules may be close to impossible for the dog to accept. After all, he's been successful so far by doing everything his way! (Patience again.) He may agree with your instruction for a few days and then slip back into his old ways, so you must be just as consistent and understanding in your teaching as you would be with a puppy. (More patience needed yet again!) Your dog has to learn to pay attention to your voice, your family, the daily routine, new smells, new sounds and, in some cases, even a new climate.

One of the most important things to find out about a newly adopted adult dog is his reaction to children (yours and others), strangers and your friends, and how he acts upon meeting other dogs. If he was not socialized with dogs as a puppy, this could be a major problem. This does not mean that he's a "bad" dog, a vicious dog or an aggressive dog; rather, it means that he has no idea how to read another dog's body language. There's no way for him to tell whether the other dog is a friend or foe. Survival instinct takes over, telling him to attack first and ask questions later. This definitely calls for professional help and, even then,

BE UPSTANDING!

You are the dog's leader. During training, stand up straight so your dog looks up at you, and therefore up to you. Say the command words distinctly, in a clear, declarative tone of voice. (No barking!) Give rewards only as the correct response takes place (remember your timing!). Praise, smiles and treats are "rewards" used to positively reinforce correct responses. Don't repeat a mistake. Just change to another exercise—you will soon find success!

may not be a behavior that can be corrected 100% reliably (or even at all). If you have a puppy, this is why it is so very important to introduce your young puppy properly to other puppies and "dog-friendly" adult dogs. You want your PWD to grow up with the breed's typical friendly outlook on life.

SHOULD WE ENROLL?

If you have the means and the time, you should definitely take your dog to obedience classes. Begin with Puppy Kindergarten classes in which puppies of all sizes learn basic lessons while getting the opportunity to meet and greet each other; it's as much about socialization as it is about good manners. What you learn in class you can practice at home. And if you goof up in practice, you'll get help in the next session.

HOUSE-TRAINING YOUR PWD

Dogs are tactility-oriented when it comes to house-training. In other words, they respond to the surface on which they are given approval to eliminate. The choice is yours (the dog's version is in parentheses): The lawn (including the neighbors' lawns)? A bare patch of earth under a tree (where people like to sit and relax in the summertime)? Concrete steps or patio (all sidewalks, garages and basement floors)? The curbside (watch out for cars)? A small area of crushed stone in a corner of the yard (mine!)? The latter is the best choice if you can manage it, because it will remain strictly for the dog's use and is easy to keep clean.

You can start out with paper-training indoors and switch over to an outdoor surface as the puppy matures and gains control over his need to eliminate. For the nay-sayers, don't worry—this won't mean that the dog will soil on every piece of newspaper lying around the house. You are training him to go outside, remember?

The PWD is a quick student and can learn to respond to hand signals; this will be of great benefit if you choose to progress to competitive obedience.

Canine Development Schedule

It is important to understand how and at what age a puppy develops into adulthood. If you are a puppy owner, consult the following Canine Development Schedule to determine the stage of development your puppy is currently experiencing. This knowledge will help you as you work with the puppy in the weeks and months ahead.

Period	Age	Characteristics
First to Third	Birth to Seven Weeks	Puppy needs food, sleep and warmth and responds to simple and gentle touching. Needs mother for security and disciplining. Needs littermates for learning and interacting with other dogs. Pup learns to function within a pack and learns pack order of dominance. Begin socializing pup with adults and children for short periods. Pup begins to become aware of his environment.
Fourth	Eight to Twelve Weeks	Brain is fully developed. Pup needs socializing with outside world. Remove from mother and littermates. Needs to change from canine pack to human pack. Human dominance necessary. Fear period occurs between 8 and 12 weeks. Avoid fright and pain.
Fifth	Thirteen to Sixteen Weeks	Training and formal obedience should begin. Less association with other dogs, more with people, places, situations. Period will pass easily if you remember this is pup's change-to-adolescence time. Be firm and fair. Flight instinct prominent. Permissiveness and over-disciplining can do permanent damage. Praise for good behavior.
Juvenile	Four to Eight Months	Another fear period about 7 to 8 months of age. It passes quickly, but be cautious of fright and pain. Sexual maturity reached. Dominant traits established. Dog should understand sit, down, come and stay by now.

Note: These are approximate time frames. Allow for individual differences in puppies.

EXTRA! EXTRA!

The headlines read: "Puppy Piddles Here!" Breeders commonly use newspapers to line their whelping pens, so puppies learn to associate newspapers with relieving themselves. Do not use newspapers to line your pup's crate, as this will signal to your puppy that it is OK to urinate in his crate. If you choose to paper-train your puppy, you will layer newspapers on a section of the floor near the door he uses to go outside. You should encourage the puppy to use the papers to relieve himself, and bring him there whenever you see him getting ready to go. Little by little, you will reduce the size of the newspaper-covered area so that the puppy will learn to relieve himself "on the other side of the door."

Starting out by paper-training often is the only choice for a city dog.

When Your Puppy's "Got to Go"

Your puppy's need to relieve himself is seemingly non-stop, but signs of improvement will be seen each week. From 8 to 10 weeks old, the puppy will have to be taken outside every time he wakes up, about 10–15 minutes after every meal and after every period of play—all day long, from first thing in the morning until his bedtime! That's a total of ten or more trips per day to teach the puppy where it's okay to relieve himself. With that schedule in mind, you can see that house-training a young puppy is not a part-time job. It requires someone to be home all day.

If that seems overwhelming or impossible, do a little planning. For example, plan to pick up your puppy at the start of a vacation period. If you can't get home in the middle of the day, plan to hire a dog-sitter or ask a neighbor to come over to take the pup outside, feed him his lunch and then take him out again about ten or so minutes after he's eaten. Also make arrangements with that or another person to be your "emergency" contact if you have to stay late on the job. Remind yourself—repeatedly—that this hectic schedule improves as the puppy gets older.

Home within a Home

Your PWD puppy needs to be confined to one secure, puppy-proof area when no one is able to watch his every move. Generally the kitchen is the place of choice because the floor is washable. Likewise, it's a busy family area that will accustom the pup to a variety of noises, everything from pots and pans to the telephone, blender and dishwasher. He will also be enchanted by the smell of your cooking (and will never be critical when you burn something). An exercise pen (also called an "ex-pen," a puppy version of a playpen) within the room of choice is an excellent means of confinement for a young pup. He can see out and has a certain amount of space in which to run about, but he is safe from dangerous things like electrical cords, heating units, trash baskets or open kitchen-supply cabinets. Place the pen where the puppy will not get a blast of heat or air conditioning.

In the pen, you can put a few toys, his bed (which can be his crate if the dimensions of pen and crate are compatible) and a few layers of newspaper in one small corner, just in case. A water bowl can be hung at a convenient height on the side of the ex-pen so it won't become a splashing pool for an innovative puppy. His food dish can go on the floor, near but not under the water bowl.

Crates are something that pet owners are at last getting used to for their dogs. Wild or domestic canines have always preferred to

DAILY SCHEDULE

How many relief trips does your puppy need per day? A puppy up to the age of 14 weeks will need to go outside about 8 to 12 times per day! You will have to take the pup out any time he starts sniffing around the floor or turning in small circles, as well as after naps, meals, games and lessons or whenever he's released from his crate. Once the puppy is 14 to 22 weeks of age, he will require only 6 to 8 relief trips. At the ages of 22 to 32 weeks, the puppy will require about 5 to 7 trips. Adult dogs typically require 4 relief trips per day, in the morning, afternoon, evening and late at night.

sleep in den-like safe spots, and that is exactly what the crate provides. How often have you seen adult dogs that choose to sleep under a table or chair even though they have full run of the house? It's the den connection.

In your "happy" voice, use the word "Crate" every time you put the pup into his den. If he's new to a crate, toss in a small biscuit for him to chase the first few times. At night, after he's been outside, he should sleep in his crate. The crate may be kept in his designated area at night or, if you want to be sure to hear those wake-up yips in the morning, put the crate in a corner of your bedroom. However, don't make any response whatsoever to whining or crying. If he's completely ignored, he'll settle down and get to sleep.

Good bedding for a young puppy is an old folded bath towel or an old blanket, something that is easily washable and disposable if necessary ("accidents" will happen!). Never put newspaper in the puppy's crate. Also, those old ideas about adding a clock to replace his mother's heartbeat, or a hot-water bottle to replace her warmth, are just that—old ideas. The clock could drive the puppy nuts, and the hot-water bottle could end up as a very soggy waterbed! An extremely good breeder would have introduced your puppy to the crate by letting two pups sleep together for a couple of nights, followed by several nights alone. How thankful you will be if you found that breeder!

Safe toys in the pup's crate or area will keep him occupied, but monitor their condition closely. Discard any toys that show signs of being chewed to bits. Squeaky parts, bits of stuffing or plastic or any other small pieces can cause

SOMEBODY TO BLAME

House-training a puppy can be frustrating for the puppy and the owner alike. The puppy does not instinctively understand the difference between defecating on the pavement outside and on the ceramic tile in the kitchen. He is confused and frightened by his human's exuberant reactions to his natural urges. The owner, arguably the more intelligent of the duo, is also frustrated that he cannot convince his puppy to obey his commands and instructions.

In frustration, the owner may struggle with the temptation to discipline the puppy, scold him or even strike him on the rear end. These forms of punishment are inappropriate and will defeat your purpose in gaining your puppy's trust and respect. Don't blame your nine-week-old puppy. Blame yourself for not being 100% consistent in the puppy's lessons and routine. The lesson here is simple: try harder and your puppy will succeed.

LEASH TRAINING

House-training and leash training go hand in hand, literally. When taking your puppy outside to do his business, lead him there on his leash. Unless an emergency potty run is called for, do not whisk the puppy up into your arms and take him outside. If you have a fenced yard, you have the advantage of letting the puppy loose to go out, but it's better to put the dog on the leash and take him to his designated place in the yard until he is reliably house-trained. Taking the puppy for a walk is the best way to house-train a dog. The dog will associate the walk with his time to relieve himself, and the exercise of walking stimulates the dog's bowels and bladder. Dogs that are not trained to relieve themselves on a walk may hold it until they get back home, which of course defeats half the purpose of the walk.

intestinal blockage or possibly choking if swallowed.

PROGRESSING WITH POTTY-TRAINING

After you've taken your puppy out and he has relieved himself in the area you've selected, he can have some free time with the family as long as there is someone responsible for watching him. That doesn't mean just someone in the same room who is watching TV or busy on the computer, but one person who is doing nothing other than keeping an eye on the pup, playing with him on the floor and helping him understand his position in the pack.

This first taste of freedom will let you begin to set the house rules. If you don't want the dog on the furniture, now is the time to prevent his first attempts to jump up onto the couch. The word to use in this case is "Off," not "Down." "Down" is the word you will use to teach the down position, which is something entirely different.

Most corrections at this stage come in the form of simply distracting the puppy. Instead of telling him "No" for "Don't chew

Whether your PWD is a pup or adult, you must be the one in control in all situations.

Happy and affectionate dogs, well-trained PWDs are among the most rewarding canine companions.

the carpet," distract the chomping puppy with a toy and he'll forget about the carpet.

As you are playing with the pup, do not forget to watch him closely and pay attention to his body language. Whenever you see him begin to circle or sniff, take the puppy outside to relieve himself. If you are paper-training, put him back into his confined area on the newspapers. In either case, praise him as he eliminates while he actually is in the act of relieving himself. Three seconds after he has finished is too late! You'll be praising him for running toward you, or picking up a toy or whatever he may be doing at that moment, and that's not what you want to be praising him for. Timing is a vital tool in all dog training. Use it.

Remove soiled newspapers immediately and replace them with clean ones. You may want to take a small piece of soiled paper and place it in the middle of the new clean papers, as the scent will attract him to that spot when it's time to go again. That scent attraction is why it's so important to clean up any messes made in the house by using a product specially made to eliminate the odor of dog urine and droppings. Regular household cleansers won't do the trick. Pet

POTTY COMMAND

Most dogs love to please their masters; there are no bounds to what dogs will do to make their owners happy. The potty command is a good example of this theory. If toileting on command makes the master happy, then more power to him. Puppies will obligingly piddle if it really makes their keepers smile. Some owners can be creative about which word they will use to command their dogs to relieve themselves. Some popular choices are "Potty," "Tinkle," "Piddle," "Let's go," "Hurry up" and "Toilet." Give the command every time your puppy goes into position and the puppy will begin to associate his business with the command.

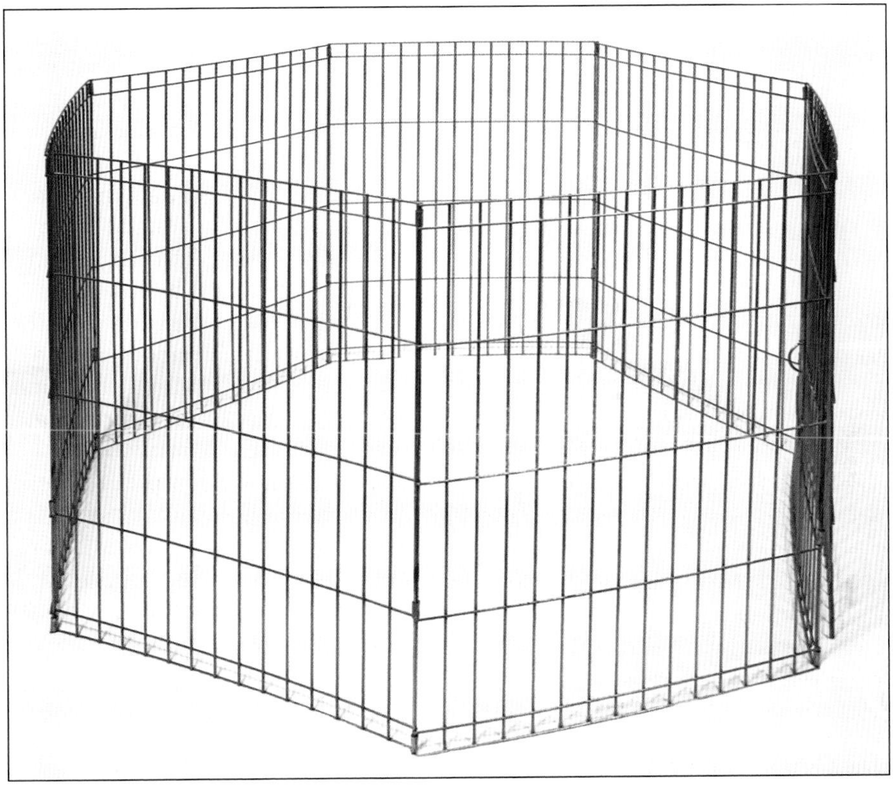

A wire pen ("ex-pen") is a helpful tool in providing your PWD pup with a place of safe confinement.

shops sell the best pet deodorizers. Invest in the largest container you can find.

Scent attraction eventually will lead your pup to his chosen spot outdoors; this is the basis of outdoor training. When you take your puppy outside to relieve himself, use a one-word command such as "Outside" or "Go-potty" (that's one word to the puppy!) as you pick him up and attach his leash. Then put him down in his area. When you notice the signs that the pup's "got to go," snap the leash on

BASIC PRINCIPLES OF DOG TRAINING

1. Start training early. A young puppy is ready, willing and able.
2. Timing is your all-important tool. Praise at the exact time that the dog responds correctly. Pay close attention.
3. Patience is almost as important as timing!
4. Repeat! The same word has to mean the same thing every time.
5. In the beginning, praise all correct behavior verbally, along with treats and petting.

quickly and lead him to his spot. Now comes the hard part—hard for you, that is. Just stand there until he urinates and defecates. Move him a few feet in one direction or another if he's just sitting there looking at you, but remember that this is neither playtime nor time for a walk. This is strictly a business trip! Then, as he circles and squats (remember your timing!), give him a quiet "Good dog" as praise. If you start to jump for joy, ecstatic over his performance, he'll do one of two things: either he will stop midstream, as it were, or he'll do it again for you—in the house—and expect you to be just as delighted!

FEAR AGGRESSION

Of the several types of aggression, the one brought on by fear is the most difficult for people to comprehend and to deal with. Aggression to protect food, or any object the dog perceives as his, is more easily understood. Fear aggression is quite different. The dog shows fear, generally for no apparent reason. He backs off, cowers or hides under the bed. If he's on lead, he will hide behind your leg and lash out unexpectedly. No matter how you approach him, he will bite. A fear-biter attacks with great speed and instantly retreats. Don't shout at him or go near him. Don't coddle, sympathize or try to protect him. To him, that's a reward. As with other forms of aggression, get professional help.

Give him five minutes or so and, if he doesn't go in that time, take him back indoors to his confined area and try again in another ten minutes, or immediately if you see him sniffing and circling. By careful observation, you'll soon work out a successful schedule.

Accidents, by the way, are just that—accidents. Clean them up quickly and thoroughly, without comment, after the puppy has been taken outside to finish his business and then put back into his area or crate. If you witness an accident in progress, say "No!" in a stern voice and get the pup outdoors immediately. No punishment is needed. You and your puppy are just learning each other's language, and sometimes it's easy to miss a puppy's message. Chalk it up to experience and watch more closely from now on.

KEEPING THE PACK ORDERLY

Discipline is a form of training that brings order to life. For example, military discipline is what allows the soldiers in an army to work as one. Discipline is a form of teaching and, in dogs, is the basis of how the successful pack operates. Each member knows his place in the pack and all respect the leader, or Alpha dog. It is essential for your puppy that you establish this type of relationship, with you as the Alpha, or leader.

TIPS FOR TRAINING AND SAFETY

1. Whether on- or off-leash, practice only in a fenced area.
2. Remove the training collar when the training session is over.
3. Don't try to break up a dogfight.
4. "Come," "Leave it" and "Wait" are safety commands.
5. The dog belongs in a crate or behind a barrier when riding in the car.
6. Don't ignore the dog's first sign of aggression. Aggression only gets worse, so take it seriously.
7. Keep the faces of children and dogs separated.
8. Pay attention to what the dog is chewing.
9. Keep the vet's number near your phone.
10. "Okay" is a useful release command.

It is a form of social coexistence that all canines recognize and accept. Discipline, therefore, is never to be confused with punishment. When you teach your puppy how you want him to behave, and he behaves properly and you praise him for it, you are disciplining him with a form of positive reinforcement.

For a dog, rewards come in the form of praise, a smile, a cheerful tone of voice, a few friendly pats or a rub of the ears. Rewards are also small food treats. Obviously, that does not mean bits of regular dog food. Instead, treats are very small bits of special things like cheese or pieces of soft dog treats. The idea is to reward the dog with something very small that he can taste and swallow, providing instant positive reinforcement. If he has to take time to chew the treat, he will have forgotten what he did to earn it by the time he is finished!

Your puppy should never be physically punished. The displeasure shown on your face and in your voice is sufficient to signal to the pup that he has done something wrong. He wants to please everyone higher up on the social ladder, especially his leader, so a scowl and harsh voice will take care of the error. Growling out the word "Shame!" when the pup is caught in the act of doing something wrong is better than the repetitive "No." Some dogs hear

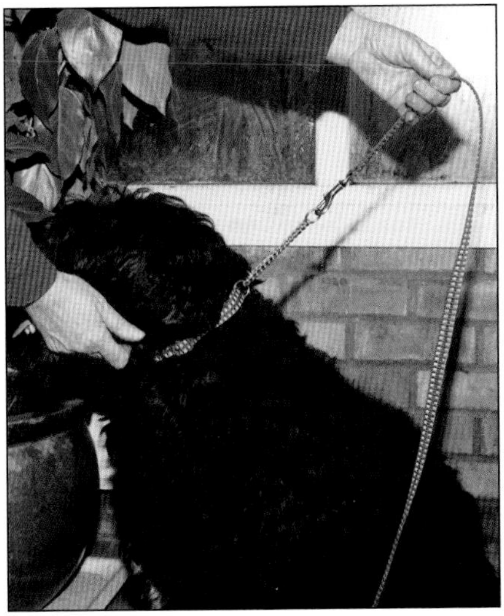

The collar and lead you choose for your Portuguese Water Dog should be sturdy yet light, and comfortable for both you and the dog.

"No" so often that they begin to think it's their name! By the way, do not use the dog's name when you're correcting him. His name is reserved to get his attention for something pleasant about to take place.

There are punishments that have nothing to do with you. For example, your dog may think that chasing cats is one reason for his existence. You can try to stop it as much as you like but without success, because it's such fun for the dog. But one good hissing, spitting swipe of a cat's claws across the dog's nose will put an end to the game forever. Intervene only when your dog's eyeball is seriously at risk. Cat scratches can cause permanent damage to an innocent but annoying puppy.

TEACHER'S PET

Dogs are individuals, not robots, with many traits basic to their breed. Some, bred to work alone, are independent thinkers; others rely on you to call the shots. If you have enrolled in a training class, your instructor can offer alternative methods of training based on your individual dog's instincts and personality. You may benefit from using a different type of collar or switching to a class with different kinds of dogs.

PUPPY KINDERGARTEN

Collar and Leash

Before you begin your PWD puppy's education, he must be used to his collar and leash. Choose a collar for your puppy that is secure, but not heavy or bulky. He won't enjoy training if he's uncomfortable. A flat buckle collar is fine for everyday wear and for initial puppy training. For older dogs, there are several types of training collars such as the martingale, which is a double loop that tightens slightly around the neck, or the head collar, which is similar to a horse's halter. The traditional choke collar is too harsh for both the PWD's coat and sensitive nature.

A lightweight 6-foot woven cotton or nylon training leash is preferred by most trainers because it is easy to fold up in your hand and comfortable to hold because there is a certain amount of give to it. There are lessons where the dog will start off 6 feet away from you at the end of the leash. The leash used to take the puppy outside to

Every dog should be trained in basic obedience, but with an intelligent and tractable Portuguese Water Dog, the possibilities of further training are many! Training also serves to strengthen the bond between you and your dog.

relieve himself is shorter because you don't want him to roam away from his area. The shorter leash will also be the one to use when you walk the puppy.

If you've been wise enough to enroll in a Puppy Kindergarten training class, suggestions will be made as to the best collar and leash for your young puppy. I say "wise" because your puppy will be in a class with puppies in his age range (up to five months old) of all breeds and sizes. It's the perfect way for him to learn the right way (and the wrong way) to interact with other dogs as well as their people. You cannot teach your puppy how to interpret another dog's sign language. For a first-time puppy owner, these socialization classes are invaluable. For experienced dog owners, they are a real boon to further training.

ATTENTION

You've been using the dog's name since the minute you collected him from the breeder, so you should be able to get his attention by saying his name—with a big smile and in an excited tone of voice. His response will be the puppy equivalent of "Here I am! What are we going to do?" Your immediate response (if you haven't guessed by now) is "Good dog." Rewarding him at the moment he pays attention to you teaches him the proper way to respond when he hears his name.

EXERCISES FOR A BASIC CANINE EDUCATION

THE SIT EXERCISE

There are several ways to teach the puppy to sit. The first one is to catch him whenever he is about to sit and, as his backside nears the floor, say "Sit, good dog!" That's positive reinforcement and, if your timing is sharp, he will learn that what he's doing at that second is connected to your saying "Sit" and that you think he's clever for doing it!

Another method is to start with the puppy on his leash in front of you. Show him a treat in the palm of your right hand. Bring

READY, SIT, GO!

On your marks, get set: train! Most professional trainers agree that the sit command is the place to start your dog's formal education. Sitting is a natural posture for most dogs, and they respond to the sit exercise willingly and readily. For every lesson, begin with the sit command so that you start out on a successful note; likewise, you should practice the sit command at the end of every lesson as well, because you always want to end on a high note.

When you command your dog to sit, use the word "Sit." Do not say "Sit down," as your dog will not know whether you mean "Sit" or "Down," or maybe you mean both. Be clear in your instructions to your dog; use one-word commands and always be consistent.

your hand up under his nose and, almost in slow motion, move your hand up and back so his nose goes up in the air and his head tilts back as he follows the treat in your hand. At that point, he will have to either sit or fall over, so as his back legs buckle under, say "Sit, good dog," and then give him the treat and lots of praise. You may have to begin with your hand lightly running up his chest, actually lifting his chin up until he sits. Some (usually older) dogs require gentle pressure on their hindquarters with the left hand, in which case the dog should be on your left side. Puppies generally do not appreciate this physical dominance.

After a few times, you should be able to show the dog a treat in the open palm of your hand, raise your hand waist-high as you say "Sit" and have him sit. You will thereby have taught him two things at the same time. Both the verbal command and the motion of the hand are signals for the sit. Your puppy is watching you almost more than he is listening to you, so what you do is just as important as what you say.

Don't save any of these drills only for training sessions. Use them as much as possible at odd times during a normal day. The dog should always sit before being given his food dish. He should sit to let you go through a doorway first, when the doorbell rings or

TIME TO PLAY!

Playtime can happen both indoors and out. A young puppy is growing so rapidly that he needs sleep more than he needs a lot of physical exercise. Puppies get sufficient exercise on their own just through normal puppy activity. Monitor play with young children so you can remove the puppy when he's had enough, or calm the kids if they get too rowdy. Almost all dogs love to chase after a toy you've thrown, and you can turn your games into educational activities. Every time your PWD brings the toy back to you, say "Give it" (or "Drop it") followed by "Good dog" and throwing it again. If he's reluctant to give it to you, offer a small treat so that he drops the toy as he takes the treat. He will soon get the idea.

DOWN

"Down" is a harsh-sounding word and a submissive posture in dog body language, thus presenting two obstacles in teaching the down command. When the dog is about to flop down on his own, tell him "Good down." Pups that are not good about being handled learn better by having food lowered in front of them. A dog that trusts you can be gently guided into position. When you give the command "Down," be sure to say it sweetly!

when you stop to speak to someone on the street.

The Down Exercise

Before beginning to teach the down command, you must consider how the dog feels about this exercise. To him, "Down" is a submissive position. Being flat on the floor with you standing over him is not his idea of fun. It's up to you to let him know that, while it may not be fun, the reward of your approval is worth his effort.

Start with the puppy on your left side in a sit position. Hold the leash right above his collar in your left hand. Have an extra-special treat, such as a small piece of cooked chicken or hot dog, in your right hand. Place it at the end of the pup's nose and steadily move your hand down and forward along the ground. Hold the leash to prevent a sudden lunge for the food. As the puppy goes into the down position, say "Down" very gently.

The difficulty with this exercise is twofold: it's both the submissive aspect and the fact that most people say the word "Down" as if they were drill sergeants in charge of recruits! So issue the command sweetly, give him the treat and have the pup maintain the down position for several seconds. If he tries to get up immediately, place your hands on his shoulders and press down gently, giving him a very quiet "Good dog." As you progress with this lesson, increase the "down time" until he will hold it until you say "Okay" (his cue for release). Practice this one in the house at various times throughout the day.

By increasing the length of time during which the dog must maintain the down position, you'll find many uses for it. For example, he can lie at your feet in the vet's office or anywhere that both of you have to wait, when you are on the phone, while the family is eating and so forth. If you progress to training for competitive obedience, he'll already be all set for the exercise called the "long down."

The Stay Exercise

You can teach your PWD to stay in the sit, down and stand positions. To teach the sit/stay, have the dog sit on your left side. Hold the leash at waist level in your left hand and let the dog know

The sit/stay exercise can be taught once your PWD has mastered the basic sit command.

OKAY!

This is the signal that tells your dog that he can quit whatever he was doing. Use "Okay" to end a session on a correct response to a command. (Never end on an incorrect response.) Lots of praise follows. People use "Okay" a lot and it has other uses for dogs, too. Your dog is barking. You say, "Okay! Come!" "Okay" signals him to stop the barking activity and "Come" allows him to come to you for a "Good dog."

that you have a treat in your closed right hand. Step forward on your right foot as you say "Stay." Immediately turn and stand directly in front of the dog, keeping your right hand up high so he'll keep his eye on the treat

You can also teach your PWD to stay in the stand position. Show dogs must have a good grasp of this command before entering the ring.

hand and maintain the sit position for a count of five. Return to your original position and offer the reward.

Increase the length of the sit/stay each time until the dog can hold it for at least 30 seconds without moving. After about a week of success, move out on your right foot and take two steps before turning to face the dog. Give the "Stay" hand signal (left palm back toward the dog's head) as you leave. He gets the treat when you return and he holds the sit/stay. Increase the distance that you walk away from him before turning until you reach the length of your training leash. But don't rush it! Go back to the beginning if he moves before he should. No matter what the lesson, never be upset by having to back up for a few days. The repetition and practice are what will make your dog reliable in these commands. It won't do any good to move on to something more difficult if the command is not mastered at the easier levels. Above all, even if you do get frustrated, never let your puppy know! Always keep a positive, upbeat attitude during training, which will transmit to your dog for positive results.

The down/stay is taught in the same way once the dog is completely reliable and steady with the down command. Again, don't rush it. With the dog in the down position on your left side, step out on your right foot as you say "Stay." Return by walking around in back of the dog and into your original position. While you are training, it's okay to murmur something like "Hold on" to encourage him to stay put. When the dog will stay without moving when you are at a distance of 3 or 4 feet, begin to increase the length

COME AND GET IT!

The come command is your dog's safety signal. Until he is 99% perfect in responding, don't use the come command if you cannot enforce it. Practice on leash with treats or squeakers, or whenever the dog is running to you. Never call him to come to you if he is to be corrected for a misdemeanor. Reward the dog with a treat and happy praise whenever he comes to you.

DON'T STRESS ME OUT

Your dog doesn't have to deal with paying the bills, the daily commute, PTA meetings and the like, but, believe it or not, there's a lot of stress in a dog's world. Stress can be caused by the owner's impatient demeanor and his angry or harsh corrections. If your dog cringes when you reach for his training collar, he's stressed. An older dog is sometimes stressed out when he goes to a new home. No matter what the cause, put off all training until he's over it. If he's going through a fear period—shying away from people, trembling when spoken to, avoiding eye contact or hiding under furniture—wait to resume training. Naturally you'd also postpone your lessons if the dog were sick, and the same goes for you. Show some compassion.

of time before you return. Be sure he holds the down on your return until you say "Okay." At that point, he gets his treat—just so he'll remember for next time that it's not over until it's over.

The Come Exercise

No command is more important to the safety of your PWD than "Come." It is what you should say every single time you see the puppy running toward you: "Skipper, come! Good dog." During playtime, run a few feet away from the puppy and turn and tell him to "Come" as he is already running to you. You can go so far as to teach your puppy two things at once if you squat down and hold out your arms. As the pup gets close to you and you're saying "Good dog," bring your right arm in about waist high. Now he's also learning the hand signal, an excellent device should you be on the phone when you need to get him to come to you! You'll also both be one step ahead when you enter obedience classes.

When the puppy responds to your well-timed "Come," try it with the puppy on the training leash. This time, catch him off guard, while he's sniffing a leaf or watching a bird: "Skipper, come!" You may have to pause for a split second after his name to be sure you have his attention. If the puppy shows any sign of confusion, give the leash a mild jerk and take a couple of steps backward. Do not repeat the command. In this case, you should say "Good come" as he reaches you.

That's the number-one rule of training. Each command word is given just once. Anything more is nagging. You'll also notice that all commands are one word only. Even when they are actually two words, you say them as one.

Never call the dog to come to you—with or without his name—if you are angry or intend to correct him for some misbehavior.

When correcting the pup, you go to him. Your dog must always connect "Come" with something pleasant and with your approval; then you can rely on his response.

Puppies, like children, have notoriously short attention spans, so don't overdo it with any of the training. Keep each lesson short. Break it up with a quick run around the yard or a ball toss, repeat the lesson and quit as soon as the pup gets it right. That way, you will always end with a "Good dog."

Life isn't perfect and neither are puppies. A time will come, often around ten months of age, when he'll become "selectively deaf" or choose to "forget" his name. He may respond by wagging his tail (and even seeming to smile at you) with a look that says "Make me!" Laugh, throw his favorite toy and skip the lesson you had planned. Pups will be pups!

The Heel Exercise

The second most important command to teach, after the come, is the heel. When you are walking your growing puppy, you need to be in control. Besides, it looks terrible to be pulled and yanked down the street, and it's not much fun either. Your eight-to ten-week-old puppy will probably follow you everywhere, but that's his natural instinct, not your control over the situation. However, any time he does follow you, you can say "Heel" and be ahead of the game, as he will learn to associate this command with the action of following you before you even begin teaching him to heel.

There is a very precise, almost military, procedure for teaching your dog to heel. As with all other obedience training, begin with the dog on your left side. He will be in a very nice sit and you will have the training leash across your chest. Hold the loop and folded leash in your right hand. Pick up the slack leash above the dog in your left hand and hold it loosely at your side. Step out on your left foot as you say "Heel." If the puppy does not move, give a gentle tug or pat your left leg to get him started. If he surges ahead of you, stop and pull him back gently until he is at your side. Tell him to sit and begin again.

Walk a few steps and stop while the puppy is correctly

LET'S GO!

Many people use "Let's go" instead of "Heel" when teaching their dogs to behave on lead. It sounds more like fun! When beginning to teach the heel, whatever command you use, always step off on your left foot. That's the one next to the dog, who is on your left side, in case you've forgotten. Keep a loose leash. When the dog pulls ahead, stop, bring him back and begin again. Use treats to guide him around turns.

An ambitious pup, with his sights set on agility when he grows up, acquaints himself with the tire jump.

beside you. Tell him to sit and give mild verbal praise. (More enthusiastic praise will encourage him to think the lesson is over.) Repeat the lesson, increasing the number of steps you take only as long as the dog is heeling nicely beside you. When you end the lesson, have him hold the sit and then give him the "Okay" to let him know that this is the end of the lesson. Praise him so that he knows he did a good job.

The cure for excessive pulling (a common problem) is to stop when the dog is no more than 2 or 3 feet ahead of you. Guide him back into position and begin again. With a really determined puller, try switching to a head collar. This will automatically turn the pup's head toward you so you can bring him back easily to the heel position. Give quiet, reassuring praise every time the leash goes slack and he's staying with you.

Staying and heeling can take a lot out of a dog, so provide playtime and free-running exercise to

RIGHT CLICK ON YOUR DOG

With three clicks, the dolphin jumps through the hoop. Wouldn't it be nice to have a dog who could obey wordless commands that easily? Clicker training actually was developed by dolphin trainers and today is used on dogs with great success. You can buy a clicker at a pet shop or pet-supply outlet, and then you'll be off and clicking.

You can click your dog into learning new commands, shaping or conditioning his behavior and solving bad habits. The clicker, used in conjunction with a treat, is an extension of positive reinforcement. The dog begins to recognize your happy clicking, which becomes sufficient as a reward. The dog is conditioned to follow your hand with the clicker, just as he would follow your hand with a treat. To discourage the dog from inappropriate behavior (like jumping up or barking), you can use the clicker to set a timeframe and then click and reward the dog once he's waited the allotted time without jumping up or barking.

shake off the stress when the lessons are over. You don't want him to associate training with all work and no fun.

TAPERING OFF TIDBITS

Your dog has been watching you—and the hand that treats—throughout all of his lessons, and now it's time to break the treat habit. Begin by giving him treats at the end of each lesson only. Then start to give a treat after the end of only some of the lessons. At the end of every lesson, as well as during the lessons, be consistent with the praise. Your pup now doesn't know whether he'll get a treat or not, but he should keep performing well just in case! Finally, you will stop giving treat rewards entirely. Save them for something brand-new that you want to teach him. Keep up the praise and you'll always have a "good dog."

HOW DO I GET TO CARNEGIE HALL?

Or the National Obedience Championships? The same way you get your dog to do anything else—practice, practice, practice. It's *how* you practice that counts. Keep sessions short, varied, interesting and interspersed with active fun. A bored dog isn't learning. If you're feeling out of sorts yourself, quit for the day. Set yourself a reasonable schedule for several brief practice sessions every day and stick to it. Practice randomly throughout the day as you're doing different things around the house. Lots of praise for that good "Sit" in front of the TV or while waiting for his dinner!

OBEDIENCE CLASSES

The advantages of an obedience class are that your dog will have to learn amid the distractions of other people and dogs and that your mistakes will be quickly corrected by the trainer. Teaching your dog along with a qualified instructor and other handlers who may have more dog experience than you is another plus of the class environment. The instructor and other handlers can help you to find the most efficient way of teaching your dog a command or exercise. It's often easier to learn by other people's mistakes than your own. You will also learn all of the requirements for competitive obedience trials, in which you can earn titles and go on to advanced jumping and retrieving exercises, which are fun for many dogs. Obedience classes build the foundation needed for many other canine activities (in which we humans are allowed to participate, too!).

TRAINING FOR OTHER ACTIVITIES

Once your dog has basic obedience under his collar and is 12 months of age, you can enter the world of agility training. Dogs think agility is pure fun, like

AN AMERICAN CURVE BALL

Comedian Don Novello conceptualized a unique new "position" for a team of six Portuguese Water Dogs in San Francisco. The sextet of PWDs has been trained to retrieve baseballs from the bay outside SBC Park, where the Giants play baseball. The dogs sit on board a boat in the bay awaiting baseballs hit over the stadium walls. The retrieved balls are auctioned off at pet-charity affairs to raise funds for a local shelter called "Pets in Need." That's another unique ability with which we can credit our modern Portuguese Water Dogs!

being turned loose in an amusement park full of obstacles! In addition to agility, there are hunting activities for sporting dogs, lure-coursing events for sighthounds, go-to-ground events for terriers, racing for the Nordic sled dogs, herding trials for the shepherd breeds and tracking, which is open to all "nosey" dogs (which would include all dogs!). Of course, the best activities for thr PWD are those that give him the opportunity to get his paws wet, whether for fun or competition. For those who like to volunteer, there is the wonderful feeling of owning a therapy dog and visiting hospices, nursing homes and veterans' homes to bring smiles, comfort and companionship to those who live there.

"What's next?" The PWD is always eager to try something new.

Around the house, your PWD can be taught to do some simple chores. You might teach him to carry a basket of household items or to fetch the morning newspaper. The kids can teach the dog all kinds of tricks, from playing hide-and-seek to balancing a biscuit on his nose. A family dog is what rounds out the family. Everything he does, including cuddling with you and gazing lovingly at you, represents the bonus of owning a dog!

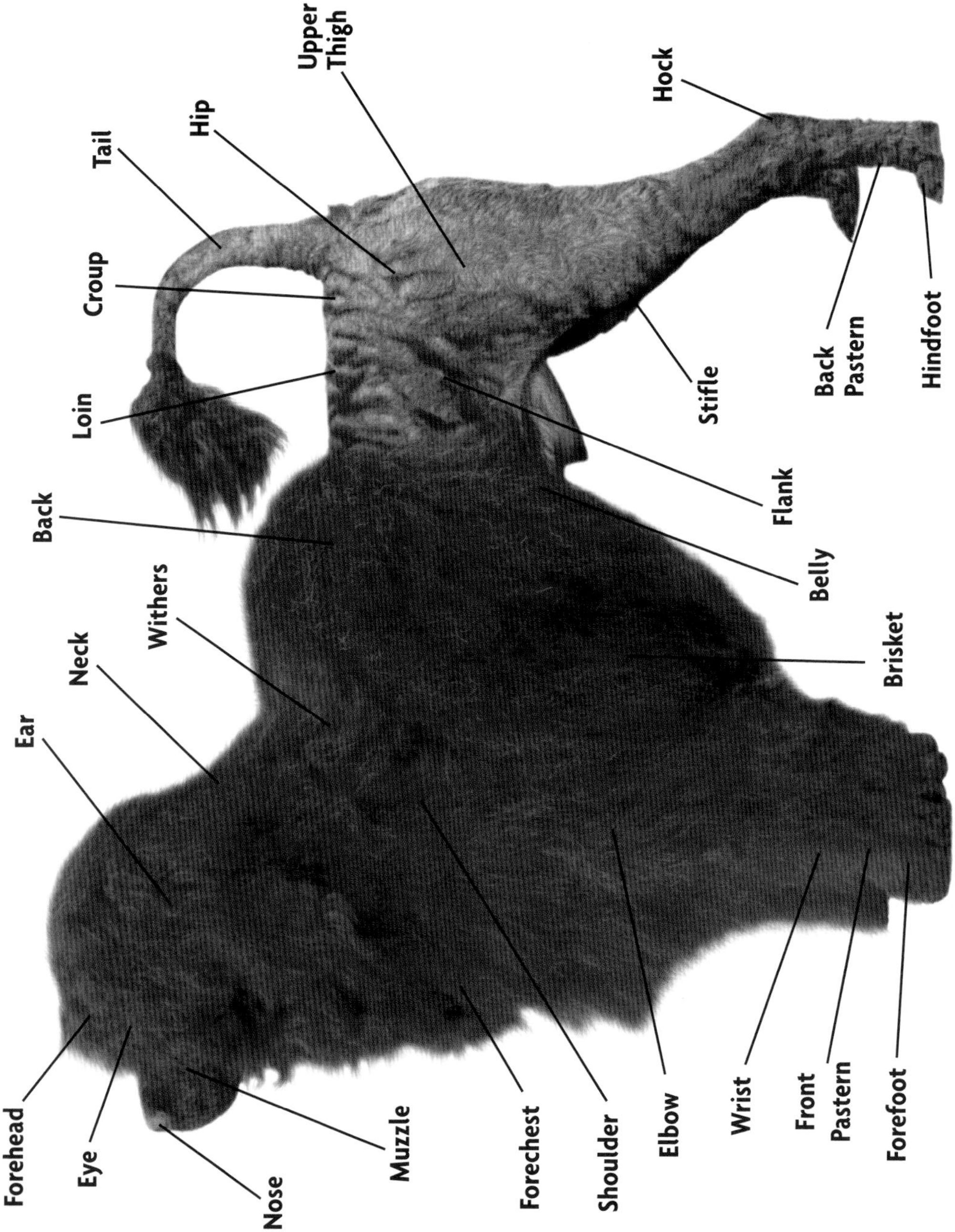

PHYSICAL STRUCTURE OF THE PORTUGUESE WATER DOG

HEALTHCARE OF YOUR
PORTUGUESE WATER DOG

BY LOWELL ACKERMAN DVM, DACVD

HEALTHCARE FOR A LIFETIME

When you own a dog, you become his healthcare advocate over his entire lifespan, as well as being the one to shoulder the financial burden of such care. Accordingly, it is worthwhile to focus on prevention rather than treatment, as you and your pet will both be happier.

Of course, the best place to have begun your program of preventive healthcare is with the initial purchase or adoption of your dog. There is no way of guaranteeing that your new furry friend is free of medical problems, but there are some things you can do to improve your odds. You certainly should have done adequate research into the PWD and have selected your puppy carefully rather than buying on impulse. Health issues aside, a large number of pet abandonment and relinquishment cases arise from a mismatch between pet needs and owner expectations. This is entirely preventable with appropriate planning and finding a good breeder.

Regarding healthcare issues specifically, it is very difficult to make blanket statements about where to acquire a problem-free pet, but, again, a reputable breeder is your best bet. In an ideal situation, you have the opportunity to see both parents, get references from other owners of the breeder's pups and see genetic-testing documentation for several generations of the litter's ancestors. At the very least, you must thoroughly investigate your breed of interest and the problems inherent in that breed, as well as the genetic testing available to screen for those problems. Genetic testing offers some important benefits, but testing is available for only a few disorders in a relatively small number of breeds and

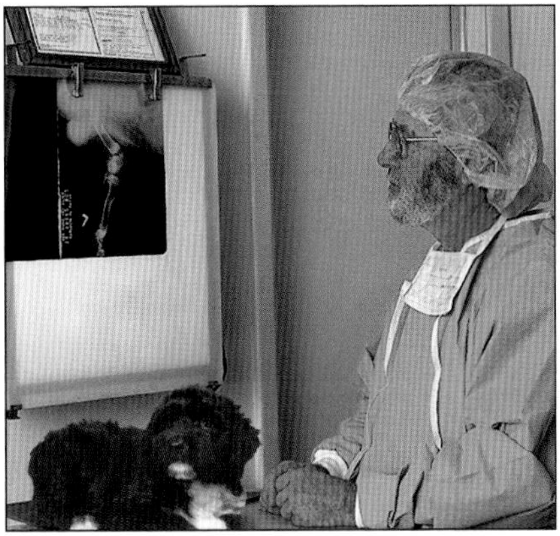

Before you buy a dog, meet and interview the veterinarians in your area. Take everything into consideration; discuss background, specialties, fees, emergency policies, etc.

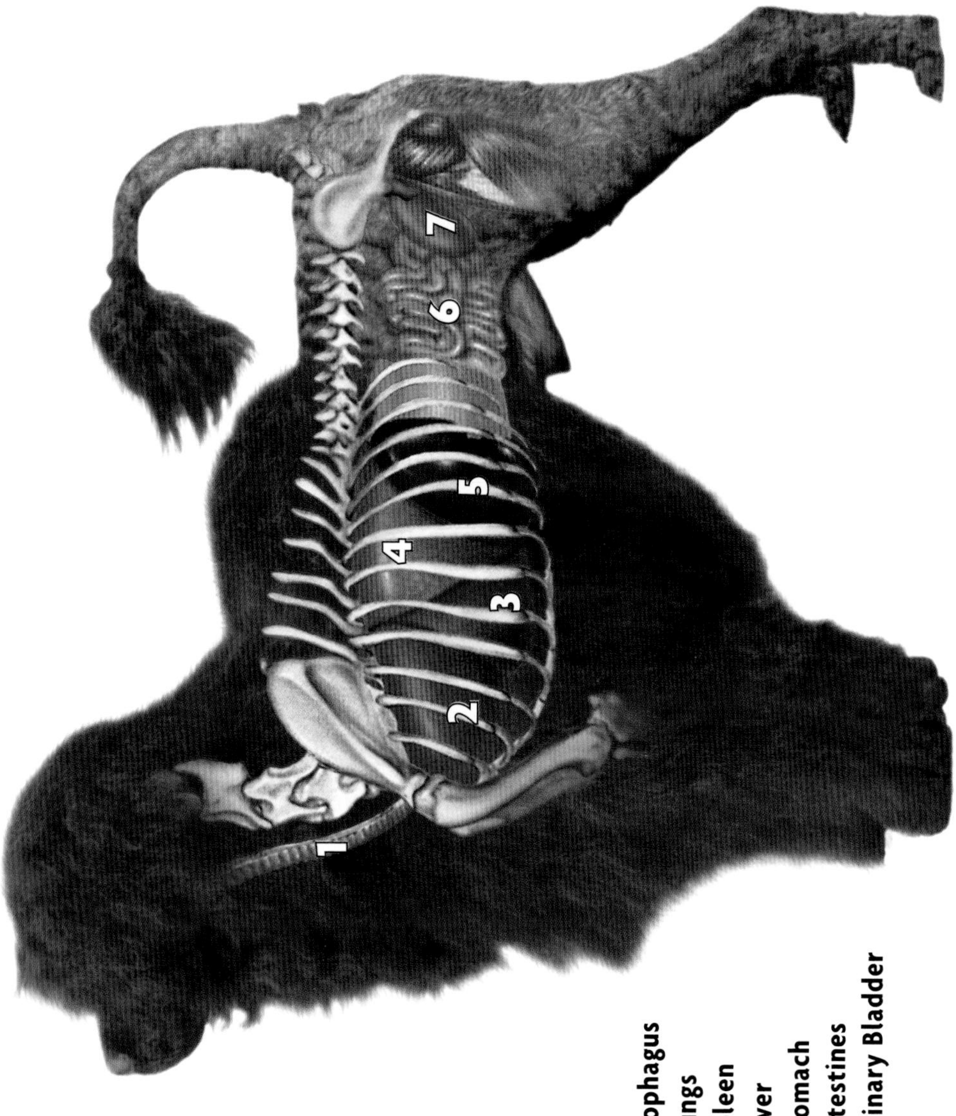

1. Esophagus
2. Lungs
3. Spleen
4. Liver
5. Stomach
6. Intestines
7. Urinary Bladder

INTERNAL ORGANS OF THE PORTUGUESE WATER DOG

is not available for some of the most common genetic diseases, such as hip dysplasia, cataracts, epilepsy, cardiomyopathy, etc. This area of research is indeed exciting and increasingly important, and advances will continue to be made each year. In fact, recent research has shown that there is an equivalent dog gene for 75% of known human genes, so research done in either species is likely to benefit the other.

We've also discussed that evaluating the behavioral nature of your PWD and that of his immediate family members is an important part of the selection process that cannot be underestimated or overemphasized. It is sometimes difficult to evaluate temperament in puppies because certain behavioral tendencies, such as some forms of aggression, may not be immediately evident. More dogs are euthanized each year for behavioral reasons than for all medical conditions combined, so it is critical to take temperament issues seriously. Start with a well-balanced, friendly companion and put the time and effort into proper socialization, and you will both be rewarded with a lifelong valued relationship.

Assuming that you have started off with a pup from healthy, sound stock, you then become responsible for helping your veterinarian keep your pet healthy. Some crucial things happen before you even bring your puppy home. Parasite control typically begins at two weeks of age, and vaccinations typically begin at six to eight weeks of age. A pre-pubertal evaluation is typically scheduled for about six months of age. At this time, a dental evaluation is done (since the adult teeth are now in),

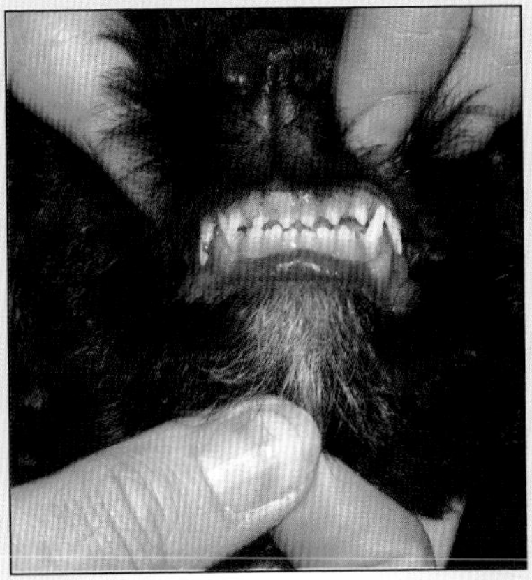

DOGGIE DENTAL DON'TS

A veterinary dental exam is necessary if you notice one or any combination of the following in your dog:

- Broken, loose or missing teeth
- Loss of appetite (which could be due to mouth pain or illness caused by infection)
- Gum abnormalities, including redness, swelling and bleeding
- Drooling, with or without blood
- Yellowing of the teeth or gumline, indicating tartar
- Bad breath

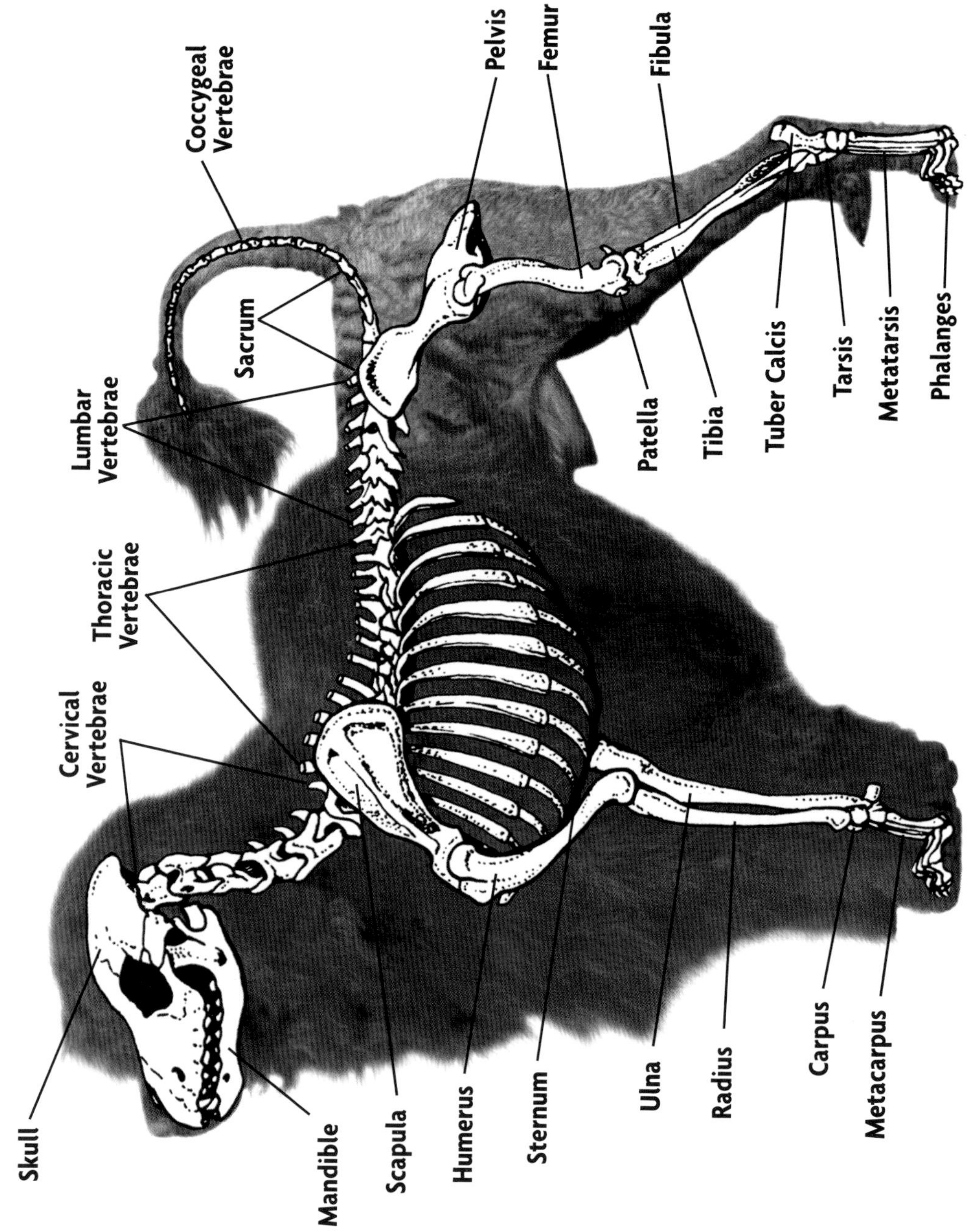

SKELETAL STRUCTURE OF THE PORTUGUESE WATER DOG

heartworm prevention is started and neutering or spaying is most commonly done.

It is critical to commence regular dental care at home if you have not already done so. It may not sound very important, but most dogs have active periodontal disease by four years of age if they don't have their teeth cleaned regularly at home, not just at their veterinary exams. Dental problems lead to more than just bad "doggie breath." Gum disease can have very serious medical consequences. If you start brushing your dog's teeth and using antiseptic rinses from a young age, your dog will be accustomed to it and will not resist. The results will be healthy dentition, which your pet will need to enjoy a long, healthy life.

Your PWD looks to you to maintain him in the best possible health.

Most dogs are considered adults at a year of age, although some larger breeds still have some filling out to do up to about two or so years old. Even individual dogs within each breed have different healthcare requirements, so work with your veterinarian to determine what will be needed and what your role should be. This doctor-client relationship is important, because as vaccination guidelines change, there may not be an annual "vaccine visit"

TAKING YOUR DOG'S TEMPERATURE

It is important to know how to take your dog's temperature at times when you think he may be ill. It's not the most enjoyable task, but it can be done without too much difficulty. It's easier with a helper, preferably someone with whom the dog is friendly, so that one of you can hold the dog while the other inserts the thermometer.

Before inserting the thermometer, coat the end with petroleum jelly. Insert the thermometer slowly and gently into the dog's rectum about one inch. Wait for the reading, about two minutes. Be sure to remove the thermometer carefully and clean it thoroughly after each use.

A dog's normal body temperature is between 100.5 and 102.5 degrees F. Immediate veterinary attention is required if the dog's temperature is below 99 or above 104 degrees F.

scheduled. You must make sure that you see your veterinarian at least annually, even if no vaccines are due, because this is the best opportunity to coordinate health-care activities and to make sure that no medical issues creep by unaddressed.

When your PWD reaches three-quarters of his anticipated lifespan, he is considered a "senior" and likely requires some special care. In general, if you've been taking great care of your canine companion throughout his formative and adult years, the transition to senior status should be a smooth one. Age is not a disease, and as long as everything is functioning as it should, there is no reason why most of late adulthood should not be rewarding for both you and your pet. This is especially true if you have tended to the details, such as regular veterinary visits, proper dental care, excellent nutrition and management of bone and joint issues.

At this stage in your PWD's life, your veterinarian may want to schedule visits twice yearly, instead of once, to run some laboratory screenings, electrocardiograms and the like, and to change the diet to something more digestible. Catching problems early is the best way to manage them effectively. Treating the early stages of heart disease is so much easier than trying to intervene when there is more significant damage to the heart muscle. Similarly, managing the beginning of

IT'S TIME TO VISIT THE VET IF:

- He has ingested a toxin such as antifreeze or a toxic plant; in these cases, administer first aid and call the vet right away
- His teeth are discolored, loose or missing or he has sores or other signs of infection or abnormality in the mouth
- He has been vomiting, has had diarrhea or has been constipated for over 24 hours; call immediately if you notice blood
- He has refused food for over 24 hours
- His eating habits, water intake or toilet habits have noticeably changed; if you have noticed weight gain or weight loss
- He shows symptoms of bloat, which requires *immediate* attention
- He is salivating excessively
- He has a lump in his throat
- He has a lump or bump anywhere on the body
- He is very lethargic
- He appears to be in pain or otherwise has trouble chewing or swallowing
- His skin loses elasticity

Of course, there will be other instances in which a visit to the vet is necessary; these are just some of the signs that could be indicative of serious problems that need to be caught as early as possible.

kidney problems is fairly routine if there is no significant kidney damage. Other problems, like cognitive dysfunction (similar to senility and Alzheimer's disease), cancer, diabetes and arthritis, are more common in older dogs, but all can be treated to help the dog live as many happy, comfortable years as possible. Just as in people, medical management is more effective (and less expensive) when you catch things early.

PROBLEM: AND THAT STARTS WITH "P"

Urinary tract problems more commonly affect female dogs, especially those who have been spayed. The first sign that a urinary tract problem exists usually is a strong odor from the urine or an unusual color. Blood in the urine, known as hematuria, is another sign of an infection, related to cystitis, a bladder infection, bladder cancer or a blood-clotting disorder. Urinary tract problems can also be signaled by the dog's straining while urinating, experiencing pain during urination and genital discharge as well as excessive water intake and urination.

Excessive drinking, in and of itself, does not indicate a urinary tract problem. A dog who is drinking more than normal may have a kidney or liver problem, a hormonal disorder or diabetes mellitus. Behaviorists report a disorder known as psychogenic polydipsia, which manifests itself in excessive drinking and urination. If you notice your dog drinking much more than normal, take him to the vet.

SELECTING A VETERINARIAN

There is probably no more important decision that you will make regarding your pet's healthcare than the selection of his doctor. Your pet's veterinarian will be a pediatrician, family-practice physician and gerontologist, depending on the dog's life stage, and will be the individual who makes recommendations regarding issues such as when specialists need to be consulted, when diagnostic testing and/or therapeutic intervention is needed and when you will need to seek outside emergency and critical-care services. Your vet will act as your advocate and liaison throughout these processes.

Everyone has his own idea about what to look for in a vet, an individual who will play a big role in his dog's (and, of course, his own) life for many years to come. For some, it is the compassionate caregiver with whom they hope to develop a professional relationship to span the lifetime of their dogs and even their future pets. For others, they are seeking a clinician with keen diagnostic and therapeutic insight who can deliver state-of-the-art healthcare. Still others need a veterinary facility that is open evenings and weekends, or is in close proximity or provides mobile veterinary services, to accommodate their schedules; these people may not much mind that their dogs might see different veterinarians on each visit. Just as we have different reasons for selecting our own healthcare professionals (e.g., covered by insurance plan, expert in field, convenient location, etc.), we should not expect that there is a one-size-fits-all recommendation for selecting a veterinarian and veterinary practice. The best advice is to be honest in your assessment of what you expect from a veterinary practice and to conscientiously research the options in your area. You will quickly appreciate that not all veterinary practices are the same, and you will be happiest with one that truly meets your needs.

There is another point to be considered in the selection of veterinary services. Not that long ago, a single veterinarian would attempt to manage all medical and surgical issues as they arose. That was often problematic, because veterinarians are trained in many species and many diseases, and it was just impossible for general veterinary practitioners to be experts in every species, every field and every ailment. However, just as in the human healthcare fields, specialization has allowed general practitioners to concentrate on primary healthcare delivery, especially wellness and the prevention of infectious diseases, and to utilize a network of specialists to assist in the management of conditions that require specific expertise and experience. Thus there are now many types of veterinary specialists, including dermatologists, cardiologists, ophthalmologists, surgeons, internists, oncologists, neurologists, behaviorists, criticalists and others to help primary-care veterinarians deal with complicated medical challenges. In most cases, specialists see cases referred by primary-care veterinarians, make diagnoses and set up management plans. From there, the animals' ongoing care is returned to their primary-care veterinarians. This important team approach to your pet's medical-care needs has provided opportunities for advanced care and an unparalleled level of quality to be delivered.

With all of the opportunities for your PWD to receive high-quality veterinary medical care, there is another topic that needs to be addressed at the same time—cost. It's been said that you can have excellent healthcare or inexpensive healthcare, but never both; this is as true in veterinary medicine as it is in human medicine. While veterinary costs are a fraction of what the same services cost in the human healthcare arena, it is still difficult to deal with unanticipated medical costs, especially since they can easily creep into hundreds or even thousands of dollars if specialists or emergency services become involved. However, there are ways of managing these risks. The easiest is to buy pet health insurance and realize that its foremost purpose is not to cover routine healthcare visits but rather to serve as an umbrella for those rainy days when your pet needs medical care and you don't want to worry about whether or not you can afford that care.

Pet insurance policies are very cost-effective (and very inexpensive by human health-insurance standards), but make sure that you buy the policy long before you intend to use it (preferably starting in puppyhood, because coverage will exclude pre-existing conditions) and that you are actually buying an indemnity insurance plan from an insurance company that is regulated by your state or province. Many insurance policy look-alikes are actually discount clubs that are redeemable only at specific locations and for specific services. An indemnity plan covers your pet at almost all veterinary, specialty and emergency practices and is an excellent way to manage your pet's ongoing healthcare needs.

Sample Vaccination Schedule

6–8 weeks of age	Parvovirus, Distemper, Adenovirus-2 (Hepatitis)
9–11 weeks of age	Parvovirus, Distemper, Adenovirus-2 (Hepatitis)
12–14 weeks of age	Parvovirus, Distemper, Adenovirus-2 (Hepatitis)
16–20 weeks of age	Rabies
1 year of age	Parvovirus, Distemper, Adenovirus-2 (Hepatitis), Rabies

Revaccination is performed every one to three years, depending on the product, the method of administration and the patient's risk. Initial adult inoculation (for dogs at least 16 weeks of age in which a puppy series was not done or could not be confirmed) is two vaccinations, done three to four weeks apart, with revaccination according to the same criteria mentioned. Other vaccines are given as decided between owner and veterinarian.

VACCINATIONS AND INFECTIOUS DISEASES

There has never been an easier time to prevent a variety of infectious diseases in your dog, but the advances we've made in veterinary medicine come with a price—choice. Now while it may seem that choice is a good thing (and it is), it has never been more difficult for the pet owner (or the veterinarian) to make an informed decision about the best way to protect pets through vaccination.

Years ago, it was just accepted that puppies got a starter series of vaccinations and then annual "boosters" throughout their lives to keep them protected. As more and more vaccines became available, consumers wanted the convenience of having all of that protection in a single injection. The result was "multivalent" vaccines that crammed a lot of protection into a single syringe. The manufacturers' recommendations were to give the vaccines annually, and this was a simple enough protocol to follow. However, as veterinary medicine has become more sophisticated

DISEASE REFERENCE CHART

	WHAT IS IT?	WHAT CAUSES IT?	SYMPTOMS
Leptospirosis	Severe disease that affects the internal organs; can be spread to people.	A bacterium, which is often carried by rodents, that enters through mucous membranes and spreads quickly throughout the body.	Range from fever, vomiting and loss of appetite in less severe cases to shock, irreversible kidney damage and possibly death in most severe cases.
Rabies	Potentially deadly virus that infects warm-blooded mammals.	Bite from a carrier of the virus, mainly wild animals.	1st stage: dog exhibits change in behavior, fear. 2nd stage: dog's behavior becomes more aggressive. 3rd stage: loss of coordination, trouble with bodily functions.
Parvovirus	Highly contagious virus, potentially deadly.	Ingestion of the virus, which is usually spread through the feces of infected dogs.	Most common: severe diarrhea. Also vomiting, fatigue, lack of appetite.
Canine cough	Contagious respiratory infection.	Combination of types of bacteria and virus. Most common: *Bordetella bronchiseptica* bacteria and parainfluenza virus.	Chronic cough.
Distemper	Disease primarily affecting respiratory and nervous system.	Virus that is related to the human measles virus.	Mild symptoms such as fever, lack of appetite and mucus secretion progress to evidence of brain damage, "hard pad."
Hepatitis	Virus primarily affecting the liver.	Canine adenovirus type I (CAV-1). Enters system when dog breathes in particles.	Lesser symptoms include listlessness, diarrhea, vomiting. More severe symptoms include "blue-eye" (clumps of virus in eye).
Coronavirus	Virus resulting in digestive problems.	Virus is spread through infected dog's feces.	Stomach upset evidenced by lack of appetite, vomiting, diarrhea.

and we have started looking more at healthcare quandaries rather than convenience, it became necessary to reevaluate the situation and deal with some tough questions. It is important to realize that whether or not to use a particular vaccine depends on the risk of contracting the disease against which it protects, the severity of the disease if it is contracted, the duration of immunity provided by the vaccine, the safety of the product and the needs of the individual animal. In a very general sense, rabies, distemper, hepatitis and parvovirus are considered core vaccine needs, while parainfluenza, *Bordetella bronchiseptica*, leptospirosis, coronavirus and borreliosis (Lyme disease) are considered non-core needs and best reserved for animals that demonstrate reasonable risk of contracting the diseases.

NEUTERING/SPAYING

Sterilization procedures (neutering for males/spaying for females) are meant to accomplish several purposes. While the underlying premise is to address the risk of pet overpopulation, there are also some medical and behavioral benefits to the surgeries as well. For females, spaying prior to the first estrus (heat cycle) leads to a marked reduction in the risk of mammary cancer. There also will be no manifestations of "heat" to attract male dogs and no bleeding in the house. For males, there is prevention of testicular cancer and a reduction in the risk of prostate problems. In both sexes, there may be some limited reduction in aggressive behaviors toward other dogs, and some diminishing of urine marking, roaming and mounting.

While neutering and spaying do indeed prevent animals from contributing to pet overpopulation, even no-cost and low-cost neutering options have not eliminated the problem. Perhaps one of the main reasons for this is that individuals that intentionally breed their dogs and those that allow their animals to run at large are the main causes of unwanted offspring. Also, animals in shelters are often there because they were abandoned or relinquished, not because they came from unplanned matings. Neutering/spaying is important, but it should be considered in the context of the real causes of animals' ending up in shelters and eventually being euthanized.

One of the important considerations regarding neutering is that it is a surgical procedure. This sometimes gets lost in discussions of low-cost procedures and commoditization of the process. In females, spaying is specifically referred to as an ovariohysterectomy. In this procedure, a midline incision is made in the abdomen and the entire uterus and both ovaries are surgically removed. While this is a major invasive surgical procedure, it usually has few complications, because it is typically performed on healthy young animals. However, it is major surgery, as any woman who has had a hysterectomy will attest.

In males, neutering has traditionally referred to castration, which involves the surgical removal of both testicles. While still a significant piece of surgery, there is not the abdominal exposure that is required in the female surgery. In addition, there is now a chemical sterilization option, in which a solution is injected into each testicle, leading to atrophy of the sperm-producing cells. This can typically be done under sedation rather than full anesthesia. This is a relatively new approach, and there are no long-term clinical studies yet available.

Neutering/spaying is typically done around six months of age at most veterinary hospitals, although techniques have been pioneered to perform the procedures in animals as young as eight weeks of age. In general, the surgeries on the very young animals are done for the specific reason of sterilizing them before they go to their new homes. This is done in some shelter hospitals for assurance that the animals will definitely not produce any pups. Otherwise, these organizations need to rely on owners to comply with their wishes to have the animals "altered" at a later date, something that does not always happen.

There are some exciting immunocontraceptive "vaccines" currently under development, and there may be a time when contraception in pets will not require surgical procedures. We anxiously await these developments.

BEWARE THE SPIDER

Should you worry about having a spider spinning her mucilaginous web over your dog? Like other venomous critters, spiders can bite dogs and cause severe reactions. The most deleterious eight-leggers are the black and red widow spiders, brown recluse and common brown spiders, whose bites can cause local pain, cramping, spasms and restlessness. These signals tell owners there is a problem, as the bites themselves can be difficult to locate under your dog's coat. Another vicious arachnid is the bark scorpion, whose bite can cause excessive drooling, tearing, urination and defecation. Often spider and scorpion bites are misdiagnosed because vets don't recognize the signs and owners didn't witness the escape of the avenging arachnid.

Number-One Killer Disease in Dogs: CANCER

In every age, there is a word associated with a disease or plague that causes humans to shudder. In the 21st century, that word is "cancer." Just as cancer is the leading cause of death in humans, it claims nearly half the lives of dogs that die from a natural disease as well as half the dogs that die over the age of ten years.

Described as a genetic disease, cancer becomes a greater risk as the dog ages. Vets and dog owners have become increasingly aware of the threat of cancer to dogs. Statistics reveal that one dog in every five will develop cancer, the most common of which is skin cancer. Many cancers, including prostate, ovarian and breast cancer, can be avoided by spaying and neutering our dogs by the age of six months.

Early detection of cancer can save or extend a dog's life, so it is absolutely vital for owners to have their dogs examined by a qualified vet or oncologist immediately upon detection of any abnormality. Certain dietary guidelines have also proven to reduce the onset and spread of cancer. Foods based on fish rather than beef, due to the presence of Omega-3 fatty acids, are recommended. Other amino acids such as glutamine have significant benefits for canines, particularly those breeds that show a greater susceptibility to cancer.

Cancer management and treatments promise hope for future generations of canines. Since the disease is genetic, breeders should never breed a dog whose parents, grandparents and any related siblings have developed cancer. It is difficult to know whether to exclude an otherwise healthy dog from a breeding program, as the disease does not manifest itself until the dog's senior years.

RECOGNIZE CANCER WARNING SIGNS

Since early detection can possibly rescue your dog from becoming a cancer statistic, it is essential for owners to recognize the possible signs and seek the assistance of a qualified professional.

- Abnormal bumps or lumps that continue to grow
- Bleeding or discharge from any body cavity
- Persistent stiffness or lameness
- Recurrent sores or sores that do not heal
- Inappetence
- Breathing difficulties
- Weight loss
- Bad breath or odors
- General malaise and fatigue
- Eating and swallowing problems
- Difficulty urinating and defecating

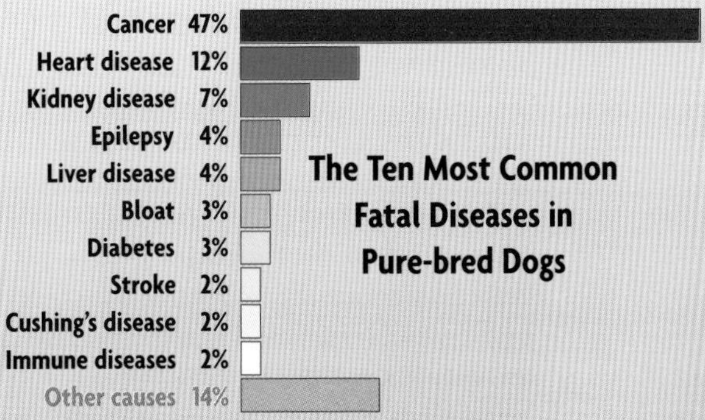

The Ten Most Common Fatal Diseases in Pure-bred Dogs

A scanning electron micrograph of a dog flea, *Ctenocephalides canis,* on dog hair

EXTERNAL PARASITES

FLEAS

Fleas have been around for millions of years and, while we have better tools now for controlling them than at any time in the past, there still is little chance that they will end up on an endangered species list. Actually, they are very well adapted to living on our pets, and they continue to adapt as we make advances.

The female flea can consume 15 times her weight in blood during active reproduction and can lay as many as 40 eggs a day. These eggs are very resistant to the effects of insecticides. They hatch into larvae, which then mature and spin cocoons. The immature fleas reside in this pupal stage until the time is right for feeding. This pupal stage is also very resistant to the effects of insecticides, and pupae can last in the environment without feeding for many months. Newly emergent fleas are attracted to animals by the warmth of the animals' bodies, movement and exhaled carbon dioxide. However, when they first emerge from their cocoons, they orient towards light; thus when an animal passes between a flea and the light source, casting a shadow, the flea pounces and starts to feed. If the animal turns out to be a dog or cat, the reproductive cycle continues. If the flea lands on another type of animal, including a person, the flea will bite but will then look for a more appropriate host. An emerging adult flea can survive without feeding for up to 12 months but, once it tastes blood, it can survive off its host for only three to four days.

It was once thought that fleas spend most of their lives in the environment, but we now know that fleas won't willingly jump off a dog unless leaping to another dog or when physically removed by brushing, bathing or other manipulation. Flea eggs, on the other hand, are shiny and smooth, and they roll off the animal and into the environment. The eggs, larvae and pupae then exist in the environment, but once the adult finds a susceptible animal, it's home sweet home until the flea is forced to seek refuge elsewhere.

Since adult fleas live on the animal and immature forms survive in the environment, a successful treatment plan must address all stages of the flea life cycle. There are now several safe and effective flea-control products that can be applied on a monthly basis. These include fipronil, imidacloprid, selamectin and permethrin (found in several formulations). Most of these products have significant flea-killing rates within 24 hours. However, none of them will control the immature forms in the environment. To accomplish this, there are a variety of insect growth regulators that can be sprayed into

FLEA PREVENTION FOR YOUR DOG

- Discuss with your veterinarian the safest product to protect your dog, likely in the form of a monthly tablet or a liquid preparation placed on the back of the dog's neck.
- For dogs suffering from flea-bite dermatitis, a shampoo or topical insecticide treatment is required.
- Your lawn and property should be sprayed with an insecticide designed to kill fleas and ticks that lurk outdoors.
- Using a flea comb, check the dog's coat regularly for any signs of parasites.
- Practice good housekeeping. Vacuum floors, carpets and furniture regularly, especially in the areas that the dog frequents, and wash the dog's bedding weekly.
- Follow up house-cleaning with carpet shampoos and sprays to rid the house of fleas at all stages of development. Insect growth regulators are the safest option.

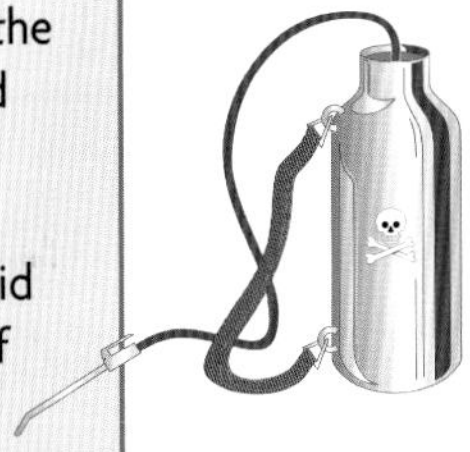

THE FLEA'S LIFE CYCLE

What came first, the flea or the egg? This age-old mystery is more difficult to comprehend than the actual cycle of the flea. Fleas usually live only about four months. A female can lay 2,000 eggs in her lifetime.

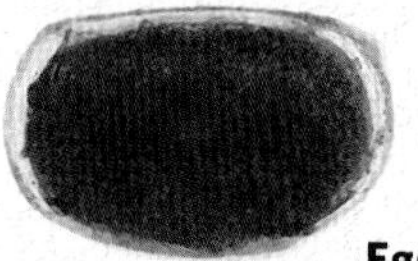

Egg

After ten days of rolling around your carpet or under your furniture, the eggs hatch into larvae, which feed on various and sundry debris. In days or months, depending on the climate, the larvae spin cocoons and develop into the pupal or nymph stage, which quickly develop into fleas.

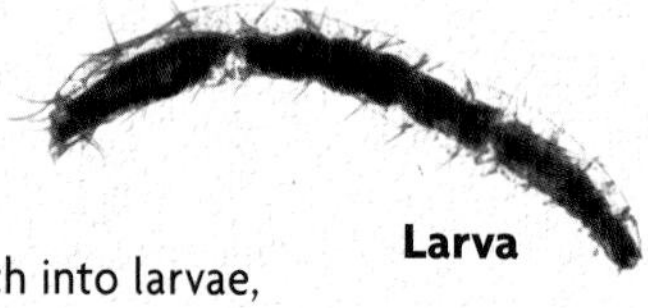

Larva

Pupa

These immature fleas must locate a host within 10 to 14 days or they will die. Only about 1% of the flea population exist as adult fleas, while the other 99% exist as eggs, larvae or pupae.

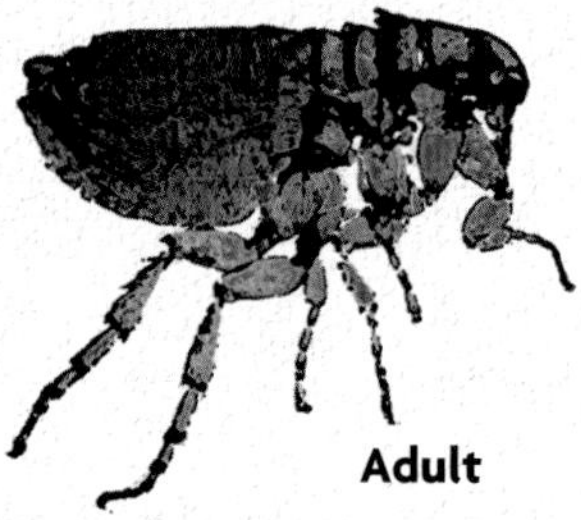

Adult

Photo by Carolina Biological Supply Co.

KILL FLEAS THE NATURAL WAY

If you choose not to go the route of conventional medication, there are some natural ways to ward off fleas:

- Dust your dog with a natural flea powder, composed of such herbal goodies as rosemary, wormwood, pennyroyal, citronella, rue, tobacco powder and eucalyptus.
- Apply diatomaceous earth, the fossilized remains of single-cell algae, to your carpets, furniture and pet's bedding. Even though it's not good for dogs, it's even worse for fleas, which will dry up swiftly and die.
- Brush your dog frequently, give him adequate exercise and let him fast occasionally. All of these activities strengthen the dog's system and make him more resistant to disease and parasites.
- Bathe your dog with a capful of pennyroyal or eucalyptus oil.
- Feed a natural diet, free of additives and preservatives. Add some fresh garlic and brewer's yeast to the dog's morning portion, as these items have flea-repelling properties.

the environment (e.g., pyriproxyfen, methoprene, fenoxycarb) as well as insect development inhibitors such as lufenuron that can be administered. These compounds have no effect on adult fleas, but they stop immature forms from developing into adults. In years gone by we relied heavily on toxic insecticides (such as organophosphates, organochlorines and carbamates) to manage the flea problem, but today's options are not only much safer to use on our pets but also safer for the environment.

TICKS

Ticks are members of the spider class (arachnids) and are blood-sucking parasites capable of transmitting a variety of diseases, including Lyme disease, ehrlichiosis, babesiosis and Rocky Mountain spotted fever. It's easy to see ticks on your own skin, but it is more of a challenge when your furry companion is affected. Whenever you happen to be planning a stroll in a tick-infested area (especially forests, grassy or wooded areas or parks) be prepared to do a thorough inspection of your dog afterward to search for ticks. Ticks can be tricky, so make sure you spend time looking in the ears, between the toes and everywhere else where a tick might hide. Ticks need to be attached for 24–72 hours before they transmit most of the diseases that they carry, so you do have a window of opportunity for some preventive intervention.

A TICKING BOMB

There is nothing good about a tick's harpooning his nose into your dog's skin. Among the diseases caused by ticks are Rocky Mountain spotted fever, canine ehrlichiosis, canine babesiosis, canine hepatozoonosis and Lyme disease. If a dog is allergic to the saliva of a female wood tick, he can develop tick paralysis.

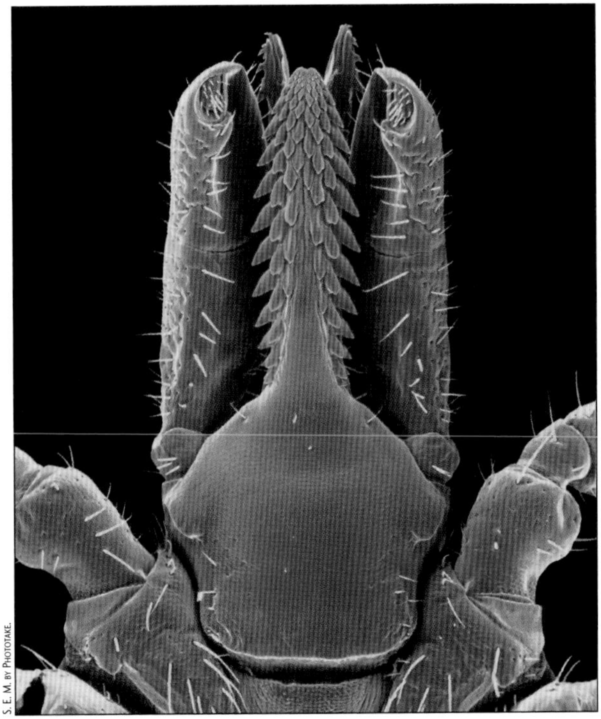

S. E. M. BY PHOTOTAKE.

A scanning electron micrograph of the head of a female deer tick, *Ixodes dammini*, a parasitic tick that carries Lyme disease.

Female ticks live to eat and breed. They can lay between 4,000 and 5,000 eggs and they die soon after. Males, on the other hand, live only to mate with the females and continue the process as long as they are able. Most ticks live on multiple hosts before parasitizing dogs. The immature forms typically reside on grass and shrubs, waiting for susceptible animals to walk by. The larvae and nymph stages typically feed on wildlife.

If only a few ticks are present on a dog, they can be plucked out, but it is important to remove the entire head and mouthparts,

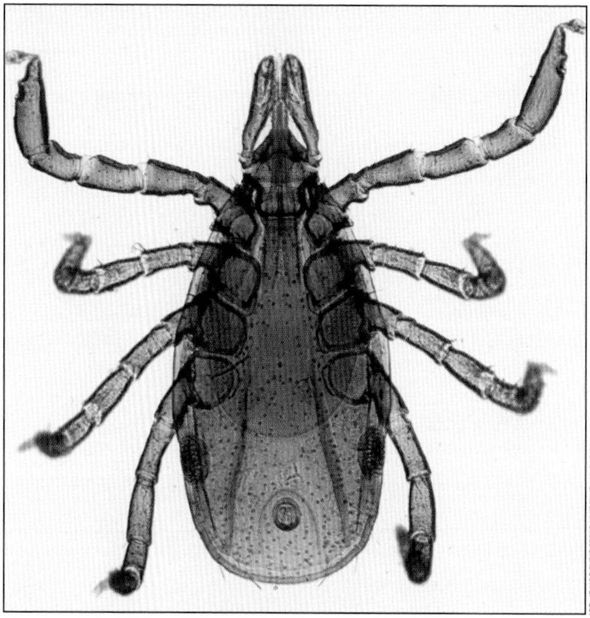

Photo by Carolina Biological Supply Co.

Deer tick, ***Ixodes dammini.***

which may be deeply embedded in the skin. This is best accomplished with forceps designed especially for this purpose; fingers can be used but should be protected with rubber gloves, plastic wrap or at least a paper towel. The tick should be grasped as closely as possible to the animal's skin and should be pulled upward with steady, even pressure. Do not squeeze, crush or puncture the body of the tick or you risk exposure to any disease carried by that tick. Once the ticks have been removed, the sites of attachment should be disinfected. Your hands should then be washed with soap and water to further minimize risk of contagion. The tick should be disposed of in a container of alcohol or household bleach.

Some of the newer flea products, specifically those with fipronil, selamectin and permethrin, have effect against some, but not all, species of tick. Flea collars containing appropriate pesticides (e.g., propoxur, chlorfenvinphos) can aid in tick control. In most areas, such collars should be placed on animals in March, at the beginning of the tick season, and changed regularly. Leaving the collar on when the pesticide level is waning invites the development of resistance. Amitraz collars are also good for tick control, and the active ingredient does not interfere with other flea-control products. The ingredient helps prevent the attachment of ticks to the skin and will cause those ticks already on the skin to detach themselves.

TICK CONTROL

Removal of underbrush and leaf litter and the thinning of trees in areas where tick control is desired are recommended. These actions remove the cover and food sources for small animals that serve as hosts for ticks. With continued mowing of grasses in these areas, the probability of ticks' surviving is further reduced. A variety of insecticide ingredients (e.g., resmethrin, carbaryl, permethrin, chlorpyrifos, dioxathion and allethrin) are registered for tick control around the home.

Mites

Mites are tiny arachnid parasites that parasitize the skin of dogs. Skin diseases caused by mites are referred to as "mange," and there are many different forms seen in dogs. These forms are very different from one another, each one warranting an individual description.

Sarcoptic mange, or scabies, is one of the itchiest conditions that affects dogs. The microscopic *Sarcoptes* mites burrow into the superficial layers of the skin and can drive dogs crazy with itchiness. They are also communicable to people, although they can't complete their reproductive cycle on people. In addition to being tiny, the mites also are often difficult to find when trying to make a diagnosis. Skin scrapings from multiple areas are examined microscopically but, even then, sometimes the mites cannot be found.

Fortunately, scabies is relatively easy to treat, and there are a variety of products that will successfully kill the mites. Since the mites can't live in the environment for very long without feeding, a complete cure is usually possible within four to eight weeks.

Cheyletiellosis is caused by a relatively large mite, which sometimes can be seen even without a microscope. Often referred to as "walking dandruff," this also causes itching, but not usually as profound as with scabies. While *Cheyletiella* mites can survive somewhat longer in the environment than scabies mites, they too are relatively easy to treat, being responsive to not only the medications used to treat scabies but also often to flea-control products.

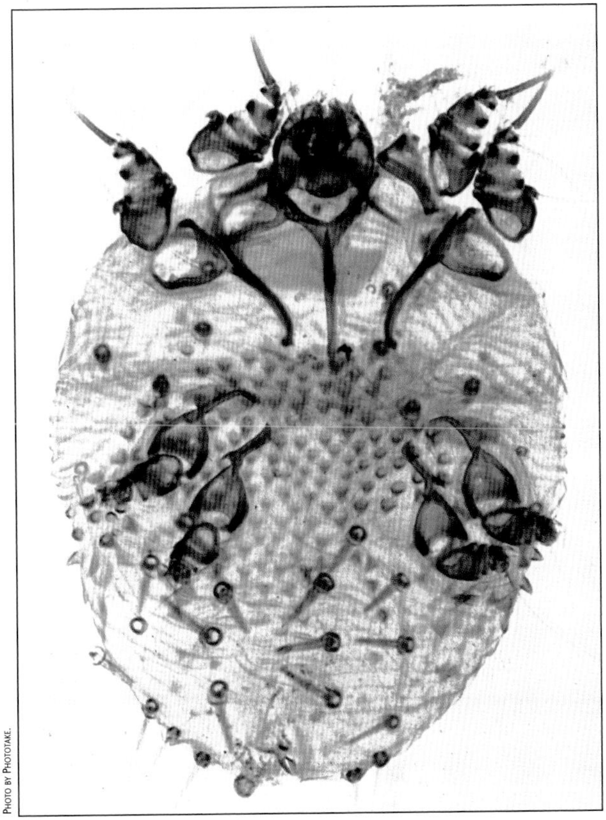

Photo by Phototake.

***Sarcoptes scabiei*, commonly known as the "itch mite."**

Otodectes cynotis is the canine ear mite and is one of the more common causes of mange, especially in young dogs in shelters or pet stores. That's because the mites are typically present in large numbers and are quickly spread to nearby animals. The mites rarely do

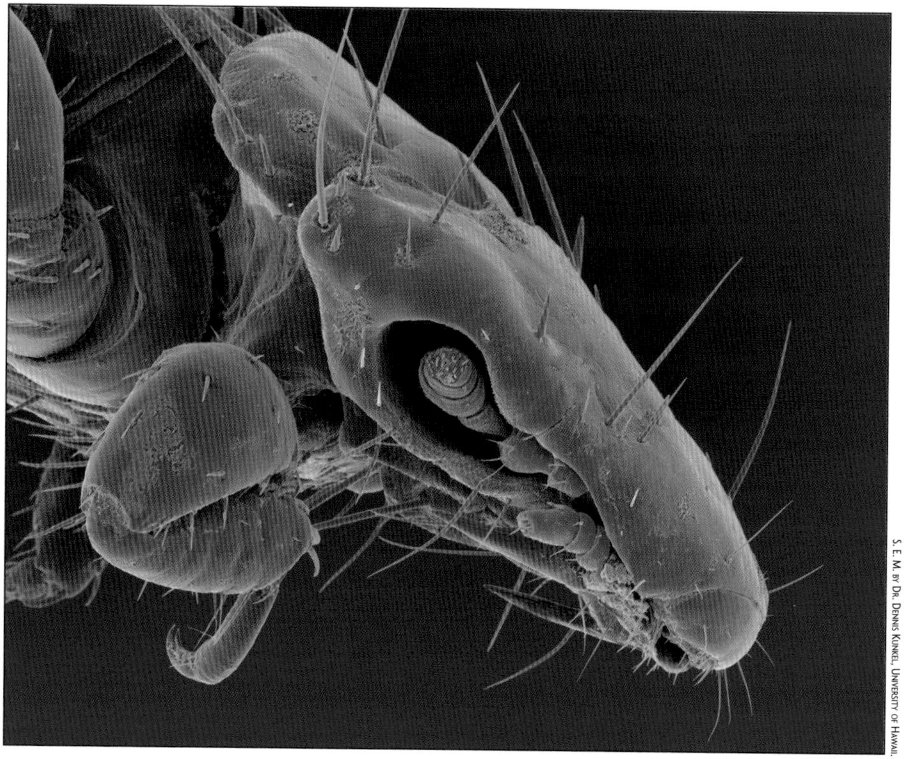

Micrograph of a dog louse, *Heterodoxus spiniger*. Female lice attach their eggs to the hairs of the dog. As the eggs hatch, the larval lice bite and feed on the blood. Lice can also feed on dead skin and hair. This feeding activity can cause hair loss and skin problems.

S. E. M. by Dr. Dennis Kunkel, University of Hawaii.

much harm but can be difficult to eradicate if the treatment regimen is not comprehensive. While many try to treat the condition with ear drops only, this is the most common cause of treatment failure. Ear drops cause the mites to simply move out of the ears and as far away as possible (usually to the base of the tail) until the insecticide levels in the ears drop to an acceptable level—then it's back to business as usual! The successful treatment of ear mites requires treating all animals in the household with a systemic insecticide, such as selamectin, or a combination of miticidal ear drops combined with whole-body flea-control preparations.

Demodicosis, sometimes referred to as red mange, can be one of the most difficult forms of mange to treat. Part of the problem has to do with the fact that the mites live in the hair follicles and they are relatively well shielded from topical and systemic products. The main issue, however, is that demodectic mange typically results only when there is some underlying process interfering with the dog's immune system.

Since *Demodex* mites are normal residents of the skin of

mammals, including humans, there is usually a mite population explosion only when the immune system fails to keep the number of mites in check. In young animals, the immune deficit may be transient or may reflect an actual inherited immune problem. In older animals, demodicosis is usually seen only when there is another disease hampering the immune system, such as diabetes, cancer, thyroid problems or the use of immune-suppressing drugs. Accordingly, treatment involves not only trying to kill the mange mites but also discerning what is interfering with immune function and correcting it if possible.

ILLUSTRATION BY PHOTOTAKE

Illustration of *Demodex folliculoram.*

Chiggers represent several different species of mite that don't parasitize dogs specifically, but do latch on to passersby and can cause irritation. The problem is most prevalent in wooded areas in the late summer and fall. Treatment is not difficult, as the mites do not complete their life cycle on dogs and are susceptible to a variety of miticidal products.

MOSQUITOES

Mosquitoes have long been known to transmit a variety of diseases to people, as well as just being biting pests during warm weather. They also pose a real risk to pets. Not only do they carry deadly heartworms but recently there also has been much concern over their involvement with West Nile virus. While we can avoid heartworm with the use of preventive medications, there are no such preventives for West Nile virus. The only method of prevention in endemic areas is active mosquito control. Fortunately, most dogs that have been exposed to the virus only developed flu-like symptoms and, to date, there have not been the large number of reported deaths in canines as seen in some other species.

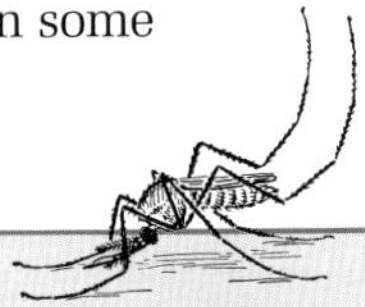

MOSQUITO REPELLENT

Low concentrations of DEET (less than 10%), found in many human mosquito repellents, have been safely used in dogs but, in these concentrations, probably give only about two hours of protection. DEET may be safe in these small concentrations, but since it is not licensed for use on dogs, there is no research proving its safety for dogs. Products containing permethrin give the longest-lasting protection, perhaps two to four weeks. As DEET is not licensed for use on dogs, and both DEET and permethrin can be quite toxic to cats, appropriate care should be exercised. Other products, such as those containing oil of citronella, also have some mosquito-repellent activity, but typically have a relatively short duration of action.

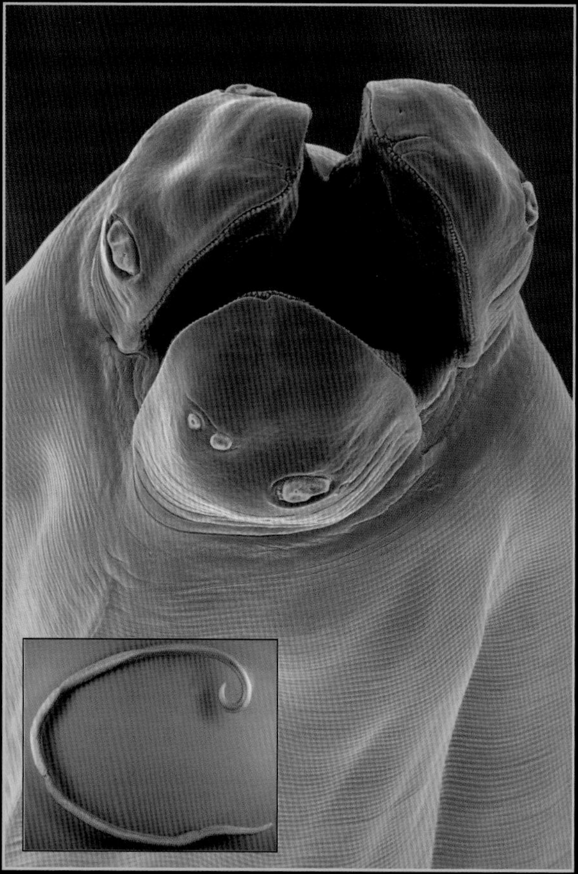

S. E. M. by Dr. Dennis Kunkel, University of Hawaii; Inset by Tam C. Nguyen.

The ascarid roundworm *Toxocara canis*, showing the mouth with three lips. INSET: Photomicrograph of the roundworm *Ascaris lumbricoides*.

ASCARID DANGERS

The most commonly encountered worms in dogs are roundworms known as ascarids. *Toxascaris leonine* and *Toxocara canis* are the two species that infect dogs. Subsisting in the dog's stomach and intestines, adult roundworms can grow to 7 inches in length and adult females can lay in excess of 200,000 eggs in a single day.

In humans, visceral larval migrans affects people who have ingested eggs of *Toxocara canis*, which frequently contaminates children's sandboxes, beaches and park grounds. The roundworms reside in the human's stomach and intestines, as they would in a dog's, but do not mature. Instead, they find their way to the liver, lungs and skin, or even to the heart or kidneys in severe cases. Deworming puppies is critical in preventing the infection in humans, and young children should never handle nursing pups who have not been dewormed.

INTERNAL PARASITES: WORMS

ASCARIDS

Ascarids are intestinal roundworms that rarely cause severe disease in dogs. Nonetheless, they are of major public health significance because they can be transferred to people. Sadly, it is children who are most commonly affected by the parasite, probably from inadvertently ingesting ascarid-contaminated soil. In fact, many yards and children's sandboxes contain appreciable numbers of ascarid eggs. So, while ascarids don't bite dogs or latch onto their intestines to suck blood, they do cause some nasty medical conditions in children and are best eradicated from our furry friends. Because pups can start passing ascarid eggs by three weeks of age, most parasite-control programs begin at two weeks of age and are repeated every two weeks until pups are eight weeks old. It is important to

HOOKED ON *ANCYLOSTOMA*

Adult dogs can become infected by the bloodsucking nematodes we commonly call hookworms via ingesting larvae from the ground or via the larvae penetrating the dog's skin. It is not uncommon for infected dogs to show no symptoms of hookworm infestation. Sometimes symptoms occur within ten days of exposure. These symptoms can include bloody diarrhea, anemia, loss of weight and general weakness. Dogs pass the hookworm eggs in their stools, which serves as the vet's method of identifying the infestation. The hookworm larvae can encyst themselves in the dog's tissues and be released when the dog is experiencing stress.

Caused by an *Ancylostoma* species whose common host is the dog, cutaneous larval migrans affects humans, causing itching and lumps and streaks beneath the surface of the skin.

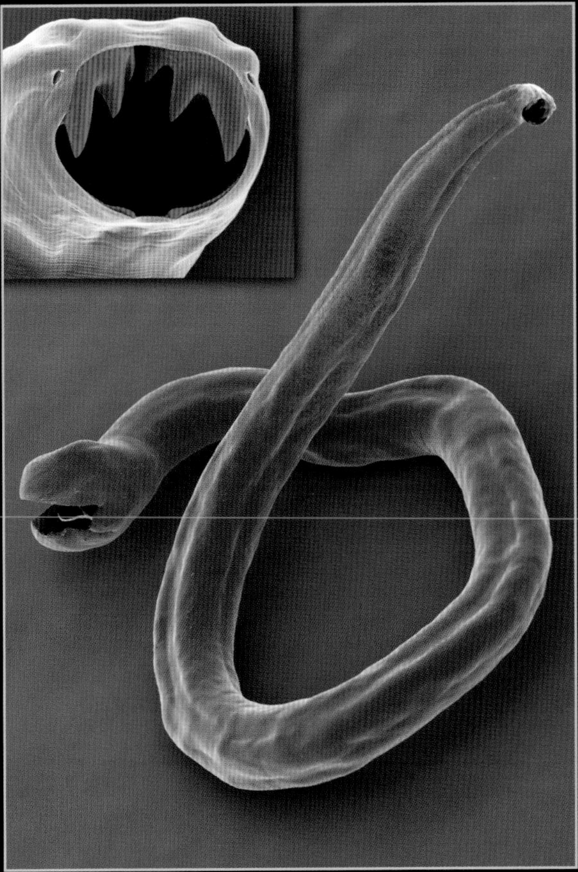

S. E. M. by Dr. Dennis Kunkel, University of Hawaii.

The hookworm *Ancylostoma caninum* infests the intestines of dogs. INSET: Note the row of hooks at the posterior end, used to anchor the worm to the intestinal wall.

realize that bitches can pass ascarids to their pups even if they test negative prior to whelping. Accordingly, bitches are best treated at the same time as the pups.

Hookworms

Unlike ascarids, hookworms do latch onto a dog's intestinal tract and can cause significant loss of blood and protein. Similar to ascarids, hookworms can be transmitted to humans, where they cause a condition known as cutaneous larval migrans. Dogs can become infected either by consuming the infective larvae or by the larvae's penetrating the skin directly. People most often get infected when they are lying on the ground (such as on a beach) and the larvae penetrate the skin. Yes, the larvae can penetrate through a beach blanket. Hookworms are typically susceptible to the same medications used to treat ascarids.

Whipworms

Whipworms latch onto the lower aspects of the dog's colon and can cause cramping and diarrhea. Eggs do not start to appear in the dog's feces until about three months after the dog was infected. This worm has a peculiar life cycle, which makes it more difficult to control than ascarids or hookworms. The good thing is that whipworms rarely are transferred to people.

Some of the medications used to treat ascarids and hookworms are also effective against whipworms, but, in general, a separate treatment protocol is needed. Since most of the medications are effective against the adults but not the eggs or larvae, treatment is typically repeated in three weeks, and then often in three months as well. Unfortunately, since dogs don't develop resistance to whipworms, it is difficult to prevent them from getting reinfected if they visit soil contaminated with whipworm eggs.

WORM-CONTROL GUIDELINES

- Practice sanitary habits with your dog and home.
- Clean up after your dog and don't let him sniff or eat other dogs' droppings.
- Control insects and fleas in the dog's environment. Fleas, lice, cockroaches, beetles, mice and rats can act as hosts for various worms.
- Prevent dogs from eating uncooked meat, raw poultry and dead animals.
- Keep dogs and children from playing in sand and soil.
- Kennel dogs on cement or gravel; avoid dirt runs.
- Administer heartworm preventives regularly.
- Have your vet examine your dog's stools at your annual visits.
- Select a boarding kennel carefully so as to avoid contamination from other dogs or an unsanitary environment.
- Prevent dogs from roaming. Obey local leash laws.

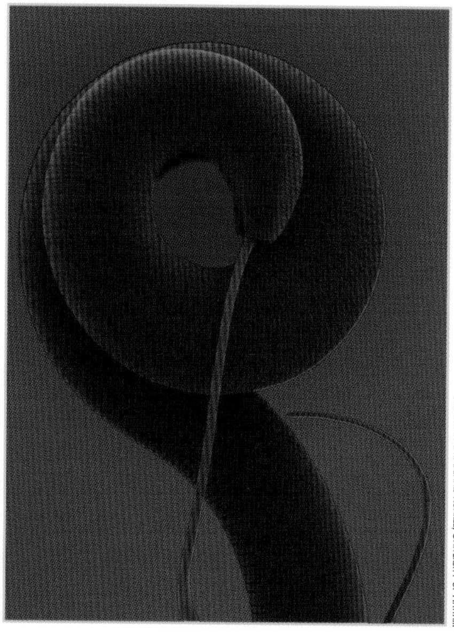
Adult whipworm, *Trichuris* sp., an intestinal parasite.

S. E. M. by Dr. Dennis Kunkel, University of Hawaii.

Tapeworms

There are many different species of tapeworm that affect dogs, but *Dipylidium caninum* is probably the most common and is spread by fleas. Flea larvae feed on organic debris and tapeworm eggs in the environment and, when a dog chews at himself and manages to ingest fleas, he might get a dose of tapeworm at the same time. The tapeworm then develops further in the intestine of the dog.

The tapeworm itself, which is a parasitic flatworm that latches onto the intestinal wall, is composed of numerous segments. When the segments break off into the intestine (as proglottids), they may accumulate around the rectum, like grains of rice. While this tapeworm is disgusting in its behavior, it is not directly communicable to humans (although humans can also get infected by swallowing fleas).

S.E.M. by Dr. Dennis Kunkel, University of Hawaii.

A dog tapeworm proglottid (body segment).

A much more dangerous flatworm is *Echinococcus multilocularis*, which is typically found in foxes, coyotes and wolves. The eggs are passed in the feces and infect rodents, and, when dogs eat the rodents, the dogs can be infected by thousands of adult tapeworms. While the parasites don't cause many problems in dogs, this is considered the most lethal worm infection that people can get. Take appropriate precautions if you live in an area in which these tapeworms are found. Do not use mulch that may contain feces of dogs, cats or wildlife, and discourage your pets from hunting wildlife. Treat these tapeworm infections aggressively in pets, because if humans get infected, approximately half die.

Heartworms

Heartworm disease is caused by the parasite *Dirofilaria immitis* and is seen in dogs around the world. A member of the roundworm group, it is spread between dogs by the bite of an infected mosquito. The mosquito injects infective larvae into the dog's skin with its bite, and these larvae develop under the skin for a period of time before making their way to the heart. There they develop into adults, which grow and create blockages of the heart, lungs and major blood vessels there. They also start producing offspring (microfilariae)

S. E. M. by Dr. Dennis Kunkel, University of Hawaii.

The dog tapeworm *Taenia pisiformis*.

A Look at Internal Parasites

Photo by Carolina Biological Supply Co.

Ascarid *Rhabditis*

Photo by Carolina Biological Supply Co.

Hookworm *Ancylostoma caninum*

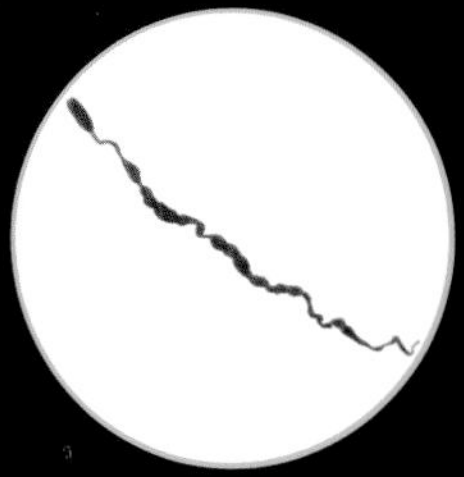

Photo by Tam C. Nguyen.

Tapeworm *Dipylidium caninum*

Photo by Tam C. Nguyen.

Heartworm *Dirofilaria immitis*

and these microfilariae circulate in the bloodstream, waiting to hitch a ride when the next mosquito bites. Once in the mosquito, the microfilariae develop into infective larvae and the entire process is repeated.

When dogs get infected with heartworm, over time they tend to develop symptoms associated with heart disease, such as coughing, exercise intolerance and potentially many other manifestations. Diagnosis is confirmed by either seeing the microfilariae themselves in blood samples or using immunologic tests (antigen testing) to identify the presence of adult heartworms. Since antigen tests measure the presence of adult heartworms and microfilarial tests measure offspring produced by adults, neither are positive until six to seven months after the initial infection. However, the beginning of damage can occur by fifth-stage larvae as early as three months after infection. Thus it is possible for dogs to be harboring problem-causing larvae for up to three months before either type of test would identify an infection.

The good news is that there are great protocols available for preventing heartworm in dogs. Testing is critical in the process, and it is important to understand the benefits as well as the limitations of such testing. All dogs six months of age or older that have not been on continuous heartworm-preventive medication

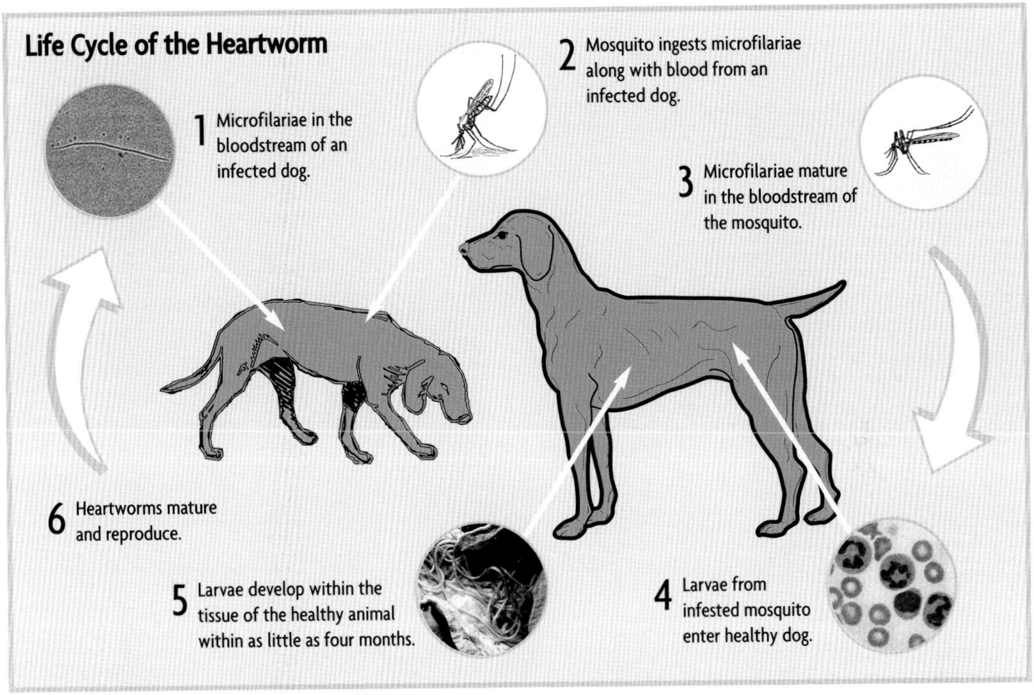

should be screened with microfilarial or antigen tests. For dogs receiving preventive medication, periodic antigen testing helps assess the effectiveness of the preventives. The American Heartworm Society guidelines suggest that annual retesting may not be necessary when owners have absolutely provided continuous heartworm prevention. Retesting on a two- to three-year interval may be sufficient in these cases. However, your veterinarian will likely have specific guidelines under which heartworm preventives will be prescribed, and many prefer to err on the side of safety and retest annually.

It is indeed fortunate that heartworm is relatively easy to prevent, because treatments can be as life-threatening as the disease itself. Treatment requires a two-step process that kills the adult heartworms first and then the microfilariae. Prevention is obviously preferable; this involves a once-monthly oral or topical treatment. The most common oral preventives include ivermectin (not suitable for some breeds), moxidectin and milbemycin oxime; the once-a-month topical drug selamectin provides heartworm protection in addition to flea, tick and other parasite controls.

THE ABCs OF Emergency Care

Abrasions
Clean wound with running water or 3% hydrogen peroxide. Pat dry with gauze and spray with antibiotic. Do not cover.

Animal Bites
Clean area with soap and saline solution or water. Apply pressure to any bleeding area. Apply antibiotic ointment.

Antifreeze Poisoning
Induce vomiting and take dog to the vet.

Bee Sting
Remove stinger and apply soothing lotion or cold compress; give antihistamine in proper dosage.

Bleeding
Apply pressure directly to wound with gauze or towel for five to ten minutes. If wound does not stop bleeding, wrap wound with gauze and adhesive tape.

Bloat/Gastric Torsion
Immediately take the dog to the vet or emergency clinic; phone from car. No time to waste.

Burns
Chemical: Bathe dog with water and pet shampoo. Rinse in saline solution. Apply antibiotic ointment.

Acid: Rinse with water. Apply one part baking soda, two parts water to affected area.

Alkali: Rinse with water. Apply one part vinegar, four parts water to affected area.

Electrical: Apply antibiotic ointment. Seek veterinary assistance immediately.

Choking
If the dog is on the verge of collapsing, wedge a solid object, such as the handle of screwdriver, between molars on one side of mouth to keep mouth open. Pull tongue out. Use long-nosed pliers or fingers to remove foreign object. Do not push the object down the dog's throat. For small or medium dogs, hold dog upside down by hind legs and shake firmly to dislodge foreign object.

Chlorine Ingestion
With clean water, rinse the mouth and eyes. Give dog water to drink; contact the vet.

Constipation
Feed dog 2 tablespoons bran flakes with each meal. Encourage drinking water. Mix ¼ teaspoon mineral oil in dog's food.

Diarrhea
Withhold food for 12 to 24 hours. Feed dog anti-diarrheal with eyedropper. When feeding resumes, feed one part boiled hamburger, one part plain cooked rice, ¼- to ¾-cup four times daily.

Dog Bite
Snip away hair around puncture wound; clean with 3% hydrogen peroxide; apply tincture of iodine. If wound appears deep, take the dog to the vet.

Frostbite
Wrap the dog in a heavy blanket. Warm affected area with a warm bath for ten minutes. Red color to skin will return with circulation; if tissues are pale after 20 minutes, contact the vet.

Use a portable, durable container large enough to contain all items

Heat Stroke
Submerge the dog in cold water; if no response within ten minutes, contact the vet.

Hot Spots
Mix 2 packets Domeboro® with 2 cups water. Saturate cloth with mixture and apply to hot spots for 15–30 minutes. Apply antibiotic ointment. Repeat every six to eight hours.

Poisonous Plants
Wash affected area with soap and water. Cleanse with alcohol. For foxtail/grass, apply antibiotic ointment.

Rat Poison Ingestion
Induce vomiting. Keep dog calm, maintain dog's normal body temperature (use blanket or heating pad). Get to the vet for antidote.

Shock
Keep the dog calm and warm; call for veterinary assistance.

Snake Bite
If possible, bandage the area and apply pressure. If the area is not conducive to bandaging, use ice to control bleeding. Get immediate help from the vet.

Tick Removal
Apply flea and tick spray directly on tick. Wait one minute. Using tweezers or wearing plastic gloves, grasp the tick's body firmly. Apply antibiotic ointment.

Vomiting
Restrict dog's water intake; offer a few ice cubes. Withhold food for next meal. Contact vet if vomiting persists longer than 24 hours.

DOG OWNER'S FIRST-AID KIT

- ❑ Gauze bandages/swabs
- ❑ Adhesive and non-adhesive bandages
- ❑ Antibiotic powder
- ❑ Antiseptic wash
- ❑ Hydrogen peroxide 3%
- ❑ Antibiotic ointment
- ❑ Lubricating jelly
- ❑ Rectal thermometer
- ❑ Nylon muzzle
- ❑ Scissors and forceps
- ❑ Eyedropper
- ❑ Syringe
- ❑ Anti-bacterial/fungal solution
- ❑ Saline solution
- ❑ Antihistamine
- ❑ Cotton balls
- ❑ Nail clippers
- ❑ Screwdriver/pen knife
- ❑ Flashlight
- ❑ Emergency phone numbers

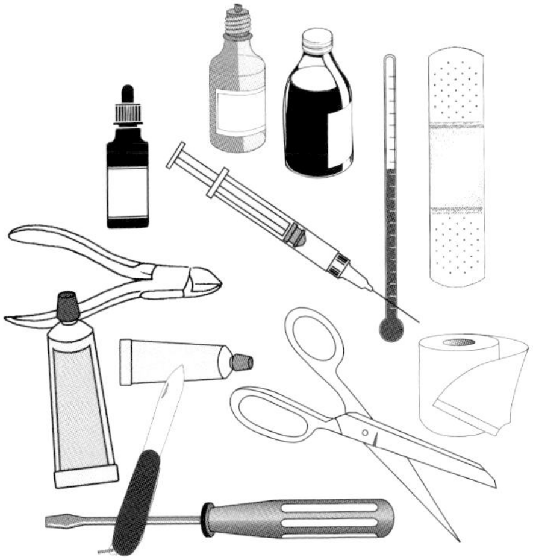

CDS: Cognitive Dysfunction Syndrome

"Old-Dog Syndrome"

There are many ways for you to evaluate old-dog syndrome. Veterinarians have defined CDS (cognitive dysfunction syndrome) as the gradual deterioration of cognitive abilities, indicated by changes in the dog's behavior. When a dog changes his routine response, and maladies have been eliminated as the cause of these behavioral changes, then CDS is the usual diagnosis.

More than half the dogs over eight years old suffer from some form of CDS. The older the dog, the more chance he has of suffering from CDS. In humans, doctors often dismiss the CDS behavioral changes as part of "winding down."

There are four major signs of CDS: frequent potty accidents inside the home, sleeping much more or much less than normal, acting confused and failing to respond to social stimuli.

Symptoms of CDS

FREQUENT POTTY ACCIDENTS

- Urinates in the house.
- Defecates in the house.
- Doesn't signal that he wants to go out.

FAILURE TO RESPOND TO SOCIAL STIMULI

- Comes to people less frequently, whether called or not.
- Doesn't tolerate petting for more than a short time.
- Doesn't come to the door when you return home.

CONFUSION

- Goes outside and just stands there.
- Appears confused with a faraway look in his eyes.
- Hides more often.
- Doesn't recognize friends.
- Doesn't come when called.
- Walks around listlessly and without a destination.

SLEEP PATTERNS

- Awakens more slowly.
- Sleeps more than normal during the day.
- Sleeps less during the night.

YOUR SENIOR
PORTUGUESE WATER DOG

When we bring home a puppy, full of the energy and exuberance that accompanies youth, we hope for a long, happy and fulfilling relationship with the new family member. Even when we adopt an older dog, we look forward to the years of companionship ahead with a new canine friend. However, aging is inevitable for all creatures, and there will come a time when your PWD reaches his senior years and will need special considerations and attention to his care.

WHEN IS MY DOG A "SENIOR"?

In general, purebred dogs are considered to have achieved senior status when they reach 75% of their breed's average lifespan, with lifespan being based on breed size. Your PWD has an average lifespan of about 10 to 12, hopefully longer, and thus is a senior citizen at around 8 or 9.

Obviously, the old "seven dog years to one human year" theory is not exact. In puppyhood, a dog's year is actually comparable to more than seven human years, considering the puppy's rapid growth during his first year. Then, in adulthood, the ratio decreases. Regardless, the more viable rule of thumb is that the larger the dog, the shorter his expected lifespan. Of course, this can vary among individual dogs, with many living longer than expected, which we hope is the case!

WHAT ARE THE SIGNS OF AGING?

By the time your dog has reached his senior years, you will know him very well, so the physical and behavioral changes that accompany aging should be noticeable to you. Humans and dogs share the most obvious physical sign of aging: gray hair! Graying often occurs first on the muzzle and face, around the eyes. Other telltale signs are the dog's overall decrease in activity. Your older dog might be more content to nap and rest, and he may not show the same old enthusiasm when it's time to play in the yard or go for a walk. Other physical signs include significant weight loss or gain; more labored

ACCIDENT ALERT!

Just as we puppy-proof our homes for the new member of the family, we must accident-proof our homes for the older dog. You want to create a safe environment in which the senior dog can get around easily and comfortably, with no dangers. A dog that slips and falls in old age is much more prone to injury than an adult, making accident prevention even more important. Likewise, dogs are more prone to falls in old age, as they do not have the same balance and coordination that they once had. Throw rugs on hardwood floors are slippery and pose a risk; even a throw rug on a carpeted surface can be an obstacle for the senior dog. Consider putting down non-slip surfaces or confining your dog to carpeted rooms only.

movement; skin and coat problems, possibly hair loss; sight and/or hearing problems; changes in toileting habits, perhaps seeming "unhousebroken" at times; and tooth decay, bad breath or other mouth problems.

There are behavioral changes that go along with aging, too. There are numerous causes for behavioral changes. Sometimes a dog's apparent confusion results from a physical change like diminished sight or hearing. If his confusion causes him to be afraid, he may act aggressively or defensively. He may sleep more frequently because his daily walks, though shorter now, tire him out. He may begin to experience separation anxiety or, conversely, become less interested in petting and attention.

There also are clinical conditions that cause behavioral changes in older dogs. One such condition is known as cognitive dysfunction (familiarly known as "old-dog" syndrome). It can be frustrating for an owner whose dog is affected with cognitive dysfunction, as it can result in behavioral changes of all types, most seemingly unexplainable. Common changes include the dog's forgetting aspects of the daily routine, such as times to eat, go out for walks, relieve himself and the like. Along the same lines, you may take your dog out at the regular time for a potty trip and he may have no idea why he is there. Sometimes a placid dog will begin to show aggressive or possessive tendencies or, conversely, a hyperactive dog will start to "mellow out."

Disease also can be the cause of behavioral changes in senior dogs. Hormonal problems (Cushing's disease is common in older dogs), diabetes and thyroid disease can cause increased appetite, which can lead to aggression related to food guarding. It's better to be proactive with your senior dog, making more frequent trips to the vet if necessary and having bloodwork done to test for the diseases that can commonly befall older dogs.

This is not to say that, as dogs age, they all fall apart physically and become nasty in personality. The aforementioned changes are discussed to alert owners to the things that may happen as their dogs get older. Many hardy dogs remain active and alert well into old age. However, it can be frustrating and heartbreaking for owners to see their beloved dogs change physically and temperamentally. Just know that it's the same PWD under there, and that he still loves you and appreciates your care, which he needs now more than ever.

HOW DO I CARE FOR MY AGING DOG?

Again, every dog is an individual in terms of aging. Your dog might reach the estimated "senior" age for the PWD and show no signs of slowing down. However, even if he shows no outward signs of aging, he should begin a senior-care program once he reaches the determined age. He may not show it, but he's not a pup anymore! By providing him with extra attention to his veterinary care at this age, you will be practicing good preventive medicine, ensuring that the rest of your dog's life will be as long, active, happy and healthy as possible. If you do notice indications of aging, such as graying and/or changes in sleeping, eating or toileting habits, this is a sign to set up a senior-care visit with your vet right away to make sure that these changes are not related to any health problems.

To start, senior dogs should visit the vet twice yearly for exams, routine tests and overall evaluations. Many veterinarians have special screening programs especially for senior dogs that can

COPING WITH A BLIND DOG

Blindness is one of the unfortunate realities of growing old, for both dogs and humans. Owners of blind dogs should not give up hope, as most dogs adapt to their compromised state with grace and patience. A sudden loss of sight poses more stress on the dog than a gradual loss, such as that through cataracts. Some dogs may need your assistance to help them get around; others will move around seemingly uninhibited. It's important to keep things consistent in the dog's familiar enviroment. Owners may need to retrain the dog to handle some basic tasks. Teaching commands like "Wait," "Stop" and "Slow" are handy as you help the dog learn to maneuver around his world. You are now more than the team captain, you're the coach and cheerleader! If your blind dog is showing signs of depression, it is your job to encourage him and give him moral support, just as you might for a member of your family or a good friend.

include a thorough physical exam; blood test to determine complete blood count; serum biochemistry test, which screens for liver, kidney and blood problems as well as cancer; urinalysis; and dental exams. With these tests, it can be determined whether your dog has any health problems; the results also establish a baseline for your pet against which future test results can be compared.

In addition to these tests, your vet may suggest additional testing, including an EKG, tests for glaucoma and other problems of the eye, chest X-rays, screening for tumors, blood pressure test, test for thyroid function and screening for parasites and reassessment of his preventive program. Your vet also will ask you questions about your dog's diet and activity level, what you feed and the amounts that you feed. This information, along with his evaluation of the dog's overall condition, will enable him to suggest proper dietary changes, if needed.

This may seem like quite a work-up for your pet, but veterinarians advise that older dogs need more frequent attention so that any health problems can be detected as early as possible. Serious conditions like kidney disease, heart disease and cancer may not present outward symptoms, or the problem may go undetected if the symptoms are mistaken by owners as just part of the aging process.

There are some conditions more common in elderly dogs that are difficult to ignore. Cognitive dysfunction shares much in common with senility and Alzheimer's disease, and dogs are not immune. Dogs can become confused and/or disoriented, lose their house-training, have abnormal sleep-wake cycles and interact differently with their owners. Be heartened by the fact that, in some ways, there are more treatment options for dogs with cognitive dysfunction than for people with similar conditions. There is good evidence that continued stimulation in the form of games, play, training and exercise can help to maintain cognitive function. There are also medications (such as seligiline) and antioxidant-fortified senior diets that have been shown to be beneficial.

Cancer is also a condition more common in the elderly. Although lung cancer, which is a major killer in humans, is relatively rare in dogs, almost all of the cancers seen in people are also seen in pets. If pets are getting regular physical examinations, cancers are often detected early. There are a variety of cancer therapies available today, and many pets continue to live happy lives with appropriate treatment.

Degenerative joint disease, often referred to as arthritis, is another malady common to both elderly dogs and humans. A lifetime of wear and tear on joints and running around at play eventually take toll and result in stiffness and difficulty in getting around. As dogs live longer and healthier lives, it is natural that they should eventually feel some of the effects of aging. Once again, if regular veterinary care has been available, your pet was not carrying extra pounds all those years and wearing those joints out before their time. If your pet was unfortunate enough to inherit hip dysplasia, osteochondrosis dissecans, or any of the other developmental orthopedic diseases, battling the onset of degenerative joint disease was probably a longstanding goal. In any case, there are now many effective remedies for managing degenerative joint disease and a number of remarkable surgeries as well.

Aside from the extra veterinary care, there is much you can do at home to keep your older dog in good condition. The dog's diet is an important factor. If your dog's appetite decreases, he will not be getting the nutrients he needs. He also will lose weight, which is unhealthy for a dog at a proper weight. Conversely, an older dog's metabolism is slower and he usually exercises less, but he should not be allowed to become obese. Obesity in an older dog is especially risky, because extra pounds mean extra stress on the body, increasing his vulnerability to heart disease. Additionally, the extra pounds make it harder for the dog to move about.

You should discuss age-related feeding changes with your vet. For a dog who has lost interest in food, it may be suggested to try some different types of food until you find something new that the dog likes. For an obese dog, a "light" formula dog food or reducing food portions may be advised, along with exercise appropriate to his physical condition and energy level.

As for exercise, the senior dog should not be allowed to

RUBDOWN REMEDY

A good remedy for an aching dog is to give him a gentle massage each day, or even a few times a day if possible. This can be especially beneficial before your dog gets out of his bed in the morning. Just as in humans, massage can decrease pain in dogs, whether the dog is arthritic or just afflicted by the stiffness that accompanies old age. Gently massage his joints and limbs, as well as petting him on his entire body. This can help his circulation and flexibility and ease any joint or muscle aches. Massaging your dog has benefits for you, too; in fact, just petting our dogs can cause reduced levels of stress and lower our blood pressure. Massage and petting also help you find any previously undetected lumps, bumps or abnormalities. Often these are not visible and only turn up by being felt.

A DIFFICULT DECISION

The decision of whether or not to euthanize is undoubtedly the hardest that owners have to make regarding their pets. It is a very emotional decision, yet it requires much clear thinking, discussion with the vet and, of course, discussion with all family members. During this time, owners will experience many different feelings: guilt, sadness, possibly anger at over having to make this type of decision. Many times, it is hard to actually come to a decision, thinking that maybe the dog will miraculously recover or that maybe he will succumb to his illness, making the decision no longer necessary.

become a "couch potato" despite his old age. He may not be able to handle the morning run, long walks and vigorous games of fetch, but he still needs to get up and get moving. Keep up with your daily walks, but keep the distances shorter and let your dog set the pace. If he gets to the point where he's not up for walks, let him stroll around the yard. On the other hand, many dogs remain very active in their senior years, so base changes to the exercise program on your own individual dog and what he's capable of. Don't worry, your PWD will let you know when it's time to rest.

Keep up with your grooming routine as you always have. Be extra diligent about checking the skin and coat for problems. Older dogs can experience thinning coats as a normal aging process, but they can also lose hair as a result of medical problems. Some thinning is normal, but patches of baldness or the loss of significant amounts of hair is not.

Hopefully, you've been regular with brushing your dog's teeth throughout his life. Healthy teeth directly affect overall good health. We already know that bacteria from gum infections can enter the dog's body through the damaged gums and travel to the organs. At a stage in life when his organs don't function as well as they used to, you don't want anything to put additional strain on them. Clean teeth also contribute to a healthy immune system. Offering the dental-type chews in addition to toothbrushing can help, as they remove plaque and tartar as the dog chews.

Along with the same good care you've given him all of his life, pay a little extra attention to your dog in his senior years and keep up with twice-yearly trips to the vet. The sooner a problem is uncovered, the greater the chances of a full recovery.

SAYING GOODBYE

While you can help your dog live as long a life as possible, you can't help him live forever. A dog's lifespan is short when compared to that of a human, so it is inevitable that pet owners will experience loss. To many, losing a beloved dog is like losing a family member. Our dogs are part of our lives every day; they are our true loyal friends and always seem to know when it's time to comfort us, to celebrate with us or to just provide the company of a caring friend. Even whether we know that our dog is nearing his final days, we can never quite prepare for his being gone.

Many dogs live out long lives and simply die of old age. Others unfortunately are taken suddenly by illness or accident, and still others find their senior years compromised by disease and physical problems. In some of these cases, owners find themselves having to make difficult decisions.

Dog owners have many options if they want to memorialize their deceased pets. Your vet may be able to help you locate a pet cemetery if you choose this option.

EUTHANASIA

When the end comes for a beloved pet, it is a very difficult time for the owners. This time is made even more difficult when the owners are faced with making a choice regarding euthanasia, more commonly known as having a very sick or very aged dog "put to sleep" or "put down."

Euthanasia can be defined as the act of ending the life of an individual suffering from a terminal illness or an incurable condition; the word "euthanasia" has its roots in Greek, meaning "good death." Euthanasia is usually accomplished by injection or other medical means that do not cause pain to the patient.

Veterinary euthanasia means that a pet is injected with a concentrated dose of anesthesia, causing unconsciousness within a few seconds and death soon after. This process is painless for the dog; the only discomfort he may feel is the prick of the needle, the same as he would with any other injection.

When faced with the decision to euthanize, you must take many things into consideration; first and foremost, what is best for your dog? Hopefully you have a good relationship with a vet whose medical opinion you trust and with whom you can discuss your decision openly and honestly.

SHOWING YOUR

PORTUGUESE WATER DOG

Is dog showing in your blood? Are you certain that your beloved Portuguese Water Dog is flawless? You are not alone! Every loving owner thinks that his dog has no faults, or too few to mention! If you are considering entering your PWD in a dog show, here are some basic questions to ask yourself:

- Did you purchase a "show-quality" puppy from the breeder?
- Is your puppy at least six months of age?
- Does the puppy exhibit correct show type for his breed?
- Does your puppy have any disqualifying faults?
- Is your PWD registered with the American Kennel Club?
- How much time do you have to devote to training, grooming, conditioning and exhibiting your dog?
- Do you understand the rules and regulations of a dog show?
- Do you have time to learn how to show your dog properly?
- Do you have the financial resources to invest in showing your dog?
- Will you show the dog yourself or hire a professional handler?
- Do you have a vehicle that can accommodate your weekend trips to the dog shows?

AKC GROUPS
For showing purposes, the American Kennel Club divides its recognized breeds into seven groups: Working Dogs (of which the PWD is a member), Sporting Dogs, Hounds, Terriers, Toys, Non-Sporting Dogs and Herding Dogs.

Even though dog shows can be exciting and enjoyable, the sport of conformation makes great demands on the exhibitors and the dogs. Winning exhibitors live for their dogs, devoting time and money to their dogs' presentation, conditioning and training. Very few novices, even those with good dogs, will find themselves in the winners' circle, though it does happen. Don't be disheartened, though. Every exhibitor began as a novice and worked his way up to the Group ring.

Assuming that you have purchased a puppy of the correct type and quality for showing, let's begin to examine the world of showing and what's required to get started. Although the entry fee into a dog show is nominal, there are lots of other hidden costs involved with "finishing" your PWD, that is, making him a champion. Things like equipment, travel, training and conditioning all cost money. A more serious campaign will include fees for a professional handler, boarding, cross-country travel and advertising. Top-winning show dogs can represent a very considerable investment—over $100,000 has been spent in campaigning some dogs. (The investment can be less, of course, for owners who don't use professional handlers.)

Many owners, on the other hand, enter their "average" PWDs in dog shows for the fun and enjoyment of it. Dog showing makes an absorbing hobby, with many rewards for dogs and owners alike. If you're having fun, meeting other people who share your interests and enjoying the overall experience, you likely will catch the "bug." Once the dog-show bug bites, its effects can last a lifetime; it's certainly much better than a deer tick! Soon you will be envisioning yourself in the center ring at the Westminster Kennel Club Dog Show in New York City, competing for the prestigious Best in Show cup. This magical dog show is televised annually from Madison Square Garden, and the victorious dog becomes a celebrity overnight.

Visiting a dog show as a spectator is a great place to start acquainting yourself with the dog-show world. Pick up the show catalog to find out what time your breed is being shown, who is judging the breed and in which ring the classes will be held. To start, PWDs compete against other PWDs, and the winner is selected as Best of Breed by the judge. This is the procedure for each breed. At a group show, all of the Best of Breed winners go on to compete for Group One in their respective groups. For example, all Best of Breed winners in a given group compete against each other; this is done for all seven groups. Finally, all seven group winners go head to head in the ring for the Best in Show award.

BECOMING A CHAMPION

An official AKC championship of record requires that a dog accumulate 15 points under three different judges, including two "majors" under different judges. Points are awarded based on the number of dogs entered into competition, varying from breed to breed and place to place. A win of three, four or five points is considered a "major." The AKC annually assigns a schedule of points to adjust for variations that accompany a breed's popularity and the population of a given area.

What most spectators don't understand is the basic idea of conformation. A dog show is often referred to as a "conformation" show. This means that the judge should decide how each dog stacks up (conforms) to the breed standard for his given breed: how well does this Portuguese Water Dog conform to the ideal representative detailed in the standard? Ideally, this is what happens. In reality, however, this ideal often gets slighted as the judge compares PWD #1 to PWD #2. Again, the ideal is that each dog is judged based on his merits in comparison to his breed standard, not in comparison to the other dogs in the ring. It is easier for judges to compare dogs of the same breed to decide which they think is the better specimen; in the Group and Best in Show ring, however, it is very difficult to compare one breed to another, like apples to oranges. Thus the dog's conformation to the breed standard—not to mention advertising dollars and good handling—is essential to success in conformation shows. The dog described in the standard (the standard for each AKC breed is written and approved by the breed's national parent club and then submitted to the AKC for approval) is the perfect dog of that breed, and breeders keep their eye on the standard when they choose which dogs to breed, hoping to get closer and closer to the ideal with each litter.

FIVE CLASSES AT SHOWS

At most AKC all-breed shows, there are five regular classes offered: Puppy, Novice, Bred-by-Exhibitor, American-bred and Open. The Puppy Class is usually divided as 6 to 9 months of age and 9 to 12 months of age. When deciding in which class to enter your dog, whether male or female, you must carefully check the show schedule to make sure that you have selected the right class. Depending on the age of the dog, its previous first-place wins and the sex of the dog, you must make the best choice. It is possible to enter a one-year-old dog who has not won sufficient first places in any of the non-Puppy Classes, though the competition is more intense the further you progress from the Puppy Class.

Another good first step for the novice is to join a dog club. You will be astonished by the many and different kinds of dog clubs in the country, with about 5,000 clubs holding events every year. Most clubs require that prospective new members present two letters of recommendation from existing members. Perhaps you've made some friends visiting a show held by a particular club and you would like to join that club. Dog clubs may specialize in a single breed, like a local or regional PWD club, or in a specific pursuit, such as obedience, tracking or hunting tests. There are all-breed clubs for all dog enthusiasts; they sponsor special training days, seminars on topics like grooming or handling or lectures on breeding or canine genetics. There are also clubs that specialize in certain types of dogs, like herding dogs, hunting dogs, water dogs, etc.

A parent club is the national organization, sanctioned by the AKC, which promotes and safeguards its breed in the country. The Portuguese Water Dog Club of America was formed in 1972 and can be contacted on the Internet at www.pwdca.org. The parent club holds an annual national specialty show, usually in a different city each year, in which many of the country's top dogs, handlers and breeders gather to compete. At a specialty show, only members of a single breed are invited to participate. There are also group specialties, in which all members of a group are invited. For more information about dog clubs in your area, contact the PWDCA, or contact the AKC at www.akc.org on the Internet or write them at their Raleigh, NC address.

Many dog shows are held outdoors. In this case, when it rains...the show must go on!

SEAL OF EXCELLENCE

The show ring is the testing ground for a breeder's program. A championship on a dog signifies that three qualified judges have placed their seal of approval on a dog. Only dogs that have earned their championships should be considered for breeding purposes. Striving to improve the breed and reproduce sound, typical examples of the breed, breeders must breed only the best. No breeder breeds only for pet homes; they strive for the top. The goal of every program must be to better the breed, and every responsible breeder wants the prestige of producing Best in Show winners.

OTHER TYPES OF COMPETITION

In addition to conformation shows, the AKC holds a variety of other competitive events. Obedience trials, agility trials and tracking trials are open to all breeds, while water trials, hunting tests, field trials, lure coursing, herding tests and trials, earthdog tests and coonhound events are limited to specific breeds or groups of breeds. The Junior Showmanship program is offered to aspiring young handlers and their dogs, and the Canine Good

Citizen® program is an all-around good-behavior test open to all dogs, pure-bred and mixed.

Obedience Trials

Mrs. Helen Whitehouse Walker, a Standard Poodle fancier, can be credited with introducing obedience trials to the United States. In the 1930s, she designed a series of exercises based on those of the Associated Sheep, Police, Army Dog Society of Great Britain. These exercises were intended to evaluate the working relationship between dog and owner. Since those early days of the sport in the US, obedience trials have grown more and more popular, and now more than 2,000 trials each year attract over 100,000 dogs and their owners. Any dog registered with the AKC, regardless of neutering or other disqualifications that would preclude entry in conformation competition, can participate in obedience trials.

There are three levels of difficulty in obedience competition. The first (and easiest) level is the Novice, in which dogs can earn the Companion Dog (CD) title. The intermediate level is the Open level, in which the Companion Dog Excellent (CDX) title is awarded. The advanced level is the Utility level, in which dogs compete for the Utility Dog (UD) title. Classes at each level are further divided into "A" and "B," with "A" for beginners and "B" for those with more experience. In order to win a title at a given level, a dog must earn three "legs." A "leg" is accomplished when a dog scores 170 or higher (200 is a perfect score). The scoring system gets a little trickier when you understand that a dog must score more than 50% of the points available for each exercise in order to actually earn the points. Available points for each exercise range between 20 and 40.

Once he's earned the UD title, a dog can go on to win the prestigious title of Utility Dog Excellent (UDX) by winning "legs" in ten shows. Additionally, Utility Dogs who win "legs" in Open B and Utility B earn points toward the lofty title of Obedience Trial Champion (OTCh.). Established in 1977 by the AKC, this title requires a dog to earn 100 points as well as three first places in a combination of Open B and Utility B classes under three different judges. The first PWD to become an Obedience Trial Champion, Spindrift Kedge, did so in 1981, just 3 months after the breed's admittance into the AKC's Miscellaneous Class. The "brass ring" of obedience competition is the AKC's National Obedience Invitational. This is an exclusive competition for only the cream of the obedience crop. In order to qualify for the invitational, a dog must be ranked in either the top 25 all-breeds in obedience or in the top three for his breed in obedience. The title at stake here is that of National Obedience Champion (NOC).

Agility Trials

Agility trials became sanctioned by the AKC in August 1994, when the first licensed agility trials were held. Since that time, agility certainly has grown in popularity by leaps and bounds, literally! The AKC allows all registered breeds (including Miscellaneous Class breeds) to participate, providing the dog is 12 months of age or older. Agility is designed so that the handler demonstrates how well the dog can work at his side. The handler directs his dog through, over, under and around an obstacle course that includes jumps, tires, the dog walk, weave poles, pipe tunnels, collapsed tunnels and more. While working his way through the course, the dog must keep one eye and ear on the handler and the rest of his body on the course. The handler runs along with the dog, giving verbal and hand signals to guide the dog through the course.

The first organization to promote agility trials in the US was the United States Dog Agility Association, Inc. (USDAA). Established in 1986, the USDAA sparked the formation of many member clubs around the country. To participate in USDAA trials, dogs must be at least 18 months of age. The USDAA and AKC both offer titles to winning dogs, although the exercises and requirements of the two organizations differ.

Agility trials are a great way to keep your dog active, and they will keep you running, too! You should join a local agility club to learn more about the sport. These clubs offer sessions in which you

CANINE GOOD CITIZEN® PROGRAM

Have you ever considered getting your dog "certified"? The AKC's Canine Good Citizen® Program affords your dog just that opportunity. Your dog shows that he is a well-behaved canine citizen, using the basic training and good manners you have taught him, by taking a series of ten tests that illustrate that he can behave properly at home, in a public place and around other dogs. The tests are administered by participating dog clubs, colleges, 4-H clubs, Scouts and other community groups and are open to all pure-bred and mixed-breed dogs. Upon passing the ten tests, the suffix CGC is then applied to your dog's name.

The ten tests are: 1. Accepting a friendly stranger; 2. Sitting politely for petting; 3. Appearance and grooming; 4. Walking on a lead; 5. Walking through a group of people; 6. Sit, down and stay on command; 7. Coming when called; 8. Meeting another dog; 9. Calm reaction to distractions; 10. Separation from owner.

can introduce your dog to the various obstacles as well as training classes to prepare him for competition. In no time, your dog will be climbing A-frames, crossing the dog walk and flying over hurdles, all with you right beside him. Your heart will leap every time your dog jumps through the hoop—and you'll be having just as much (if not more) fun!

TRACKING

Tracking tests are exciting ways to test your PWD's instinctive scenting ability on a competitive level. All dogs have a nose, and all breeds are welcome in tracking tests. The first AKC-licensed tracking test took place in 1937 as part of the Utility level at an obedience trial, and thus competitive tracking was officially begun. The first title, Tracking Dog (TD), was offered in 1947, ten years after the first official tracking test. It was not until 1980 that the AKC added the title Tracking Dog Excellent (TDX), which was followed by the title Versatile Surface Tracking (VST) in 1995. Champion Tracker (CT) is awarded to a dog who has earned all three of those titles.

The TD level is the first and most basic level in tracking, progressing in difficulty to the TDX and then the VST. A dog must follow a track laid by a human 30 to 120 minutes prior in order to earn the TD title. The track is about 500 yards long and contains up to 5 directional changes. At the next level, the TDX, the dog must follow a 3- to 5-hour-old track over a course that is up to 1,000 yards long and has up to 7 directional changes. In the most difficult level, the VST, the track is up to 5 hours old and located in an urban setting.

WATER TRIALS

The Portuguese Water Dog is foremost a working breed. Whether he is kept in a pet home or actually used in a working capacity, his original instincts remain strong. He is a strong swimmer and retriever, showing enthusiasm for performing the tasks given to him and forming a true bond of teamwork with his master. In order to

FOR MORE INFORMATION....

For reliable up-to-date information about registration, dog shows and other canine competitions, contact one of the national registries by mail or via the Internet.

American Kennel Club
5580 Centerview Dr., Raleigh, NC 27606-3390
www.akc.org

United Kennel Club
100 E. Kilgore Road, Kalamazoo, MI 49002
www.ukcdogs.com

Canadian Kennel Club
89 Skyway Ave., Suite 100, Etobicoke, Ontario
M9W 6R4 Canada
www.ckc.ca

develop and preserve these instinctive abilities in today's dogs and future generations of PWDs, the PWDCA has implemented a water-trial program in which owners and dogs can train and compete.

PWDCA water trials are held by the club itself and its regional affiliates. Titles can be earned at each level of water-trial competition, and the exercises progress in difficulty from one level to the next. In order, starting with the easiest level, the titles available are: Junior Water Dog (JWD), Apprentice Water Dog (AWD), Working Water Dog (WWD), Courier Water Dog (CWD) and Courier Water Dog Excellent (CWDX).

The most difficult level, open to dogs that have earned the CWDX, is the Versatility level. In Versatility competition, a "package" consisting of a selection of exercises from the various levels is randomly chosen by the judge on the day of the trial. The object of Versatility is to test how well dog and handler can work together and perform the exercises with little advance notice; this is a true test of both the dog's skills and the ability of the human/dog pair to act as a team. Some of the exercises in water trials are bringing a dummy from the shore into the boat, retrieving a dummy and returning it to the boat, retrieving a fishing net, blind retrieve, transporting a gear bag and/or courier pouch and more, all simulations of tasks that the breed was bred for and has traditionally carried out in its role as a worker on the fishing boats of its native Portugal.

PURPLE AND GOLD HERITAGE

The Westminster Kennel Club show, America's most prestigious dog show, gained its name from the founders' favorite Manhattan hotel bar where they gathered to discuss their sporting ventures. Another theory about the name comes from a Pointer named Juno, who came from the kennel of the Duke of Westminster in England. Although Juno participated in the first show in 1877, the Duke's kennel name likely had less bearing on the choice of the club's name than did the gentlemen's celebrated watering hole. Juno, by the way, is not the Pointer in the Westminster symbol: that Pointer was a celebrated show dog by the name of Sensation, who was owned by the club.

Today the Westminster Kennel Club dog show is the oldest uninterrupted annual dog show in the world, and the second oldest sporting event in America. The first show was held on May 8-10, 1877 at Gilmore's Garden, the famous Hippodrome, with an entry of over 1200 dogs. Presently the show is held in the month of February at Madison Square Garden in New York City with an entry of 2,500 champion dogs and is televised nationally.

BEHAVIOR OF YOUR PORTUGUESE WATER DOG

UNDERSTANDING THE CANINE MINDSET

For starters, you and your dog are on different wavelengths. Your dog makes connections based on the fact that he lives in the present, so when he is doing something and you interrupt to dispense praise or a correction, a connection, positive or negative, is made. To the dog, that's like one plus one equals two! In the same sense, it's also easy to see that when your timing is off, you will cause an incorrect connection. The one-plus-one way of thinking is why you must never scold a dog for behavior that took place an hour, 15 minutes or even 5 seconds ago. But it is also why, when your timing is perfect, you can teach him to do all kinds of wonderful things—as soon as he has made that essential connection. What helps the process is his desire to please you and to have your approval.

There are behaviors we admire in dogs, such as friendliness and obedience, as well as those behaviors that cause problems to a varying degree. The dog owner who encounters minor behavioral problems is wise to solve them promptly or get professional help. Bad behaviors are not corrected by repeatedly shouting "No" or getting angry with the dog. Only the giving of praise and approval for good behavior lets your dog understand right from wrong. The longer a bad behavior is allowed to continue, the harder it is to overcome. A responsible breeder is often able to help. Each dog is unique, so try not to compare your dog's behavior with your neighbor's dog or the one you had as a child.

Have your veterinarian check the dog to see whether a behavior problem could have a physical cause. An earache or toothache, for example, could be the reason for a dog to snap at you if you were to touch his head when putting on his leash. A sharp correction from you would only increase the behavior. When a physical basis is eliminated, and if the problem is not something you understand or can cope with, ask for the name of a behavioral specialist, preferably one who is familiar with the PWD.

Be sure to keep the breeder informed of your progress.

Many things, such as environment and inherited traits, form the basic behavior of a dog, just as in humans. You also must factor into his temperament the purpose for which your PWD was originally bred. The major obstacle lies in the dog's inability to explain his behavior to us in a way that we understand. The one thing you should not do is to give up and abandon your dog. Somewhere a misunderstanding has occurred but, with help and patient understanding on your part, you should be able to work out the majority of bothersome behaviors.

SEPARATION ANXIETY

Any behaviorist will tell you that separation anxiety is the most common problem about which pet owners complain, and we know that the Portuguese Water Dog loves to be the center of attention. It is also one of the easiest problems to prevent. Unfortunately, a behaviorist usually is not consulted until the dog is a stressed-out, neurotic mess. At that stage, it is indeed a problem that requires the help of a professional.

Training the puppy to the fact that people in the house come and go is essential in order to avoid this anxiety. Leaving the puppy in his crate or a confined area while family members go in and out, and stay out for longer and longer periods of time, is the basic way to desensitize the pup to the family's frequent departures. If you are at home most of every day, make it a point to go out for at least an hour or two whenever possible.

How you leave is vital to the dog's reaction. Your dog is no fool. He knows the difference between sweats and business suits, jeans and dresses. He sees you pat your pocket to check for your wallet, open your briefcase, check that you have your cell phone or pick up the car keys. He knows from the hurry of the kids in the morning that they're off to school until afternoon. Lipstick? Aftershave lotion? Lunch boxes? Every move you make registers in his sensory perception and memory. Your puppy knows more about your departures than the FBI. You can't get away with a thing!

Separation anxiety is quickly becoming one of the most common problems that dog owners face, as it is often the case that no one in the household is at home all day with the family dog.

Before you got dressed, you checked the dog's water bowl and his supply of long-lasting chew toys, and you turned the radio on low. You will leave him in what he considers his "safe" area, not with total freedom of the house. If you've invested in child safety gates, you can be reasonably sure that he'll remain in the designated area. Don't give him access to a window where he can watch you leave the house. If you're leaving for an hour or two, just put him into his crate with a safe toy.

Now comes the test! You are ready to walk out the door. Do not give your PWD a big hug and a fond farewell. Do not drag out a long goodbye. Those are the very things that jump-start separation anxiety. Toss a biscuit into the dog's area, call out "So long, pooch" and close the door. You're gone. The chances are that the dog may bark a couple of times, or maybe whine once or twice, and then settle down to enjoy his biscuit and take a lovely nap, especially if you took him for a nice long walk after breakfast. As he grows up, the barks and whines will stop because it's an old routine, so why should he make the effort?

When you first brought home the puppy, the come-and-go routine was intermittent and constant. He was put into his crate with a tiny treat. You left (silently) and returned in 3 minutes, then 5, then 10, then 15, then half an hour, until finally you could leave without a problem and be gone for 2 or 3 hours. If, at any time in the future, there's a "separation" problem, refresh his memory by going back to that basic training.

Now comes the next most important part—your return. Do not make a big production of coming home. "Hi, poochie" is as grand a greeting as he needs. When you've taken off your hat and coat, tossed your briefcase on the hall table and glanced at the mail, and the dog has settled down from the excitement of seeing you "in person" from his confined area, then go and give him a warm, friendly greeting. A potty trip is needed and a walk would be appreciated, since he's been such a good dog.

AGGRESSION

"Aggression" is a word that is often misunderstood and is sometimes even used to describe what is actually normal canine behavior. For example, it's normal for puppies to growl when playing tug-of-war. It's "puppy talk." There are different forms of dog aggression, but all are degrees of dominance, indicating that the dog, not his master, is (or thinks he is) in control. When the dog feels that he (or his control of the situation) is threatened, he will respond. The extent of the

Aggression or playtime? Dogs often engage in play-fighting behavior with each other, so you must know your dog well enough to recognize when he's just playing rough or when he's being aggressive.

aggressive behavior varies with individual dogs. It is not at all pleasant to see bared teeth or to hear your dog growl or snarl, but these are signs of behavior that, if left uncorrected, can become extremely dangerous. A word of warning here: never challenge an aggressive dog. He is unpredictable and therefore unreliable to approach.

Nothing gets a "hello" from strangers on the street quicker than walking a puppy, but people should ask permission before petting your dog so you can tell him to sit in order to receive the admiring pats. If a hand comes down over the dog's head and he shrinks back, ask the person to bring their hand up, underneath the pup's chin. Now you're correcting strangers, too! But if you don't, it could make your dog afraid of strangers, which in turn can lead to fear-biting. Socialization prevents much aggression before it rears its ugly head. Fortunately, well-socialized PWDs should be friendly with all, whether human or animal.

The body language of an aggressive dog about to attack is clear. The dog will have a hard, steady stare. He will try to look as big as possible by standing stiff-legged, pushing out his chest, keeping his ears up and holding his tail up and steady. The hackles on his back will rise so that a ridge of hairs stands up. This posture may include the curled lip, snarl and/or growl, or he may be silent. He looks, and definitely is, very dangerous.

This dominant posture is seen in dogs that are territorially aggressive. Deliverymen are

Dogs who have plenty of safe chew toys will be more likely to keep themselves occupied and less likely to engage in destructive behavior.

constant victims of serious bites from such dogs. Territorial aggression is the reason you should never, ever, try to train a puppy to be a watchdog. It can escalate into this type of behavior over which you will have no control. All forms of aggression must be taken seriously and dealt with immediately. If signs of aggressive behavior continue, or grow worse, or if you are at all unsure about how to deal with your dog's behavior, get the help of a professional.

CHEWING

All puppies chew. All dogs chew. This is a fact of life for canines, and sometimes you may think it's what your dog does best! A pup starts chewing when his first set of teeth erupts and continues throughout the teething period. Chewing gives the pup relief from itchy gums and incoming teeth and, from that time on, he gets great satisfaction out of this normal, somewhat idle, canine activity. Providing safe chew toys is the best way to direct this behavior in an appropriate manner. Chew toys are available in all sizes, textures and flavors, but you must monitor the wear-and-tear inflicted on your pup's toys to be sure that the ones you've chosen are safe and remain in good condition.

Puppies cannot distinguish between a rawhide toy and a nice leather shoe or wallet. It's up to you to keep your possessions away from the dog and to keep your eye on the dog. There's a form of destruction caused by chewing that is not the dog's fault. Let's say you allow him on the sofa. One day he takes a rawhide bone up on the sofa and, in the course of chewing on the bone, takes up a bit of fabric. He continues to chew. Disaster! Now you've learned the lesson: Dogs with chew toys have to be either kept off furniture and carpets,

FOOD GUARDING

A dog's guarding his dinner dish is totally unacceptable behavior. If your dog starts to exhibit food-guarding tendencies, prevent them by putting part of his food in the dish and picking up the dish when he's finished. Replenish the dish, make him sit and offer him some food from your hand, and then put the dish down. Repeat!

carefully supervised or put into their confined areas for chew time.

The wooden legs of furniture are favorite objects for chewing. The first time, tell the dog "Leave it!" (or "No!") and offer him a chew toy as a substitute. But your clever dog may be hiding under the chair and doing some silent destruction, which you may not notice until it's too late. In this case, it's time to try one of the foul-tasting products, made specifically to prevent destructive chewing, that is sprayed on the objects of your dog's chewing attention. These products also work to keep the dog away from plants, trash, etc. It's even a good way to stop the dog from "mouthing" or chewing on your hands or the leg of your pants. (Be sure to wash your hands after the mouthing lesson!) A little spray goes a long way.

JUMPING UP

Jumping up is a device of enthusiastic, attention-seeking puppies, but adult dogs often like to jump up as well, usually as a form of canine greeting. The PWD is an exuberant breed, so owners must deal with their dogs' energetic "bounciness." Some owners wouldn't have it any other way! They encourage their dogs, and the owners and dogs alike enjoy the friendly physical contact. Some owners think that it's cute when it comes from a puppy, but not from an adult.

Conversely, there are those who consider jumping up to be one of the worst kinds of bad manners to be found in a dog; these people are likely not the best match for a PWD! Among this group inevitably are bound to be some of your best friends.

THE MACHO DOG

The Venus/Mars differences are found in dogs, too. Males have distinct behaviors that, while seemingly sex-related, are more closely connected to the role of the male as leader. Marking territory by urinating on it is one means that male dogs use to establish their presence. Doing so merely says, "I've been here." Small dogs often attempt to lift their legs higher on the tree than the previous male. While this is natural behavior outdoors on items like telephone poles, fence posts, fire hydrants and most other upright objects, marking indoors is totally unacceptable. Treat it as you would a house-training accident and clean thoroughly to eradicate the scent. Another behavior often seen in the macho male, mounting is a dominance display. Neutering the dog before six months of age helps to deter this behavior. You can discourage him from mounting by catching the dog as he's about to mount you, stepping quickly aside and saying "Off!"

DIGGING OUT

Some dogs love to dig. Others wouldn't think of it. Digging is considered "self-rewarding behavior" because it's fun! Further, a bored dog is likely to dig to occupy himself. Of all the digging solutions offered by the experts, most are only marginally successful and none is guaranteed to work. The best cure is prevention, which means removing the dog from the offending site when he digs as well as distracting him when you catch him digging so that he turns his attentions elsewhere. That means that you have to supervise your dog's yard time. An unsupervised digger can create havoc with your landscaping or, worse, run away!

There are two situations in which your dog should be restrained from any and all jumping up. One is around children, especially young children and those who are not at ease with dogs. The other is when you are entertaining guests. No one who comes dressed up for a party wants to be groped by your dog, no matter how friendly his intentions or how clean his paws.

The answer to this one is relatively simple. If the dog has already started to jump up, the first command is "Off," followed immediately by "Sit." The dog must sit every time you are about to meet a friend on the street or when someone enters your home, be it child or adult. You may have to ask people to ignore the dog for a few minutes in order to let his urge for an enthusiastic greeting subside. If your dog is too exuberant and won't sit still, you'll have to work harder by first telling him "Off" and then issuing the down/stay command. This requires more work on your part, because the down is a submissive position and your dog is only trying to be super-friendly. A small treat is expected when training for this particular down.

If you have a real pet peeve about a dog's jumping up, then disallow it from the day your puppy comes home. Jumping up is a subliminally taught human-to-dog greeting. Dogs don't greet each other in this way. It begins because your puppy is close to the ground and he's easier to pet and cuddle if he reaches up and you bend over to meet him halfway. If you won't like it later, don't start it when he is young, but do give lots of praise and affection for a good sit.

FOOD-RELATED PROBLEMS

Who can resist the bleeding-heart look that says "I'm starving," or the paw that gently pats your knee and gives you a knowing look, or the whining "please" or even the total body language of a perfect sit beneath the cookie jar. No one who professes to love his dog can turn down the pleas of his clever canine's performances every time.

One thing is for sure, though: definitely do not allow begging at the table. Family meals do not include your dog.

Control your dog's begging habit by making your dog work for his rewards. Ignore his begging when you can. Use "Off" for the pawing. A sit or even a long down will interrupt the whining. His reward in these situations is definitely not a treat! Casual verbal praise is enough. Be sure all members of the family follow the same rules. There is a different type of begging that does demand your immediate response and that is the appeal to be let (or taken) outside! Usually that is a quick paw or small whine to get your attention, followed by a race to the door. This type of begging needs your quick attention and approval. Of course, a really smart dog will soon figure out how to cut you off at the pass and direct you to that cookie jar on your way to the door! Some dogs are always one step ahead of us.

Stealing food is a problem only if you are not paying attention. A dog can't steal food that is not within his reach. Leaving your dog in the kitchen with the roast beef on the table is asking for trouble, no matter how well-trained he is. Putting cheese and crackers on the coffee table also requires a watchful eye to stop the thief in his tracks. The word to use (one word, remember, even if it's two words pronounced as one) is "Leave it!" Instead of preceding it with yet another "No," try using a guttural sound like "Aagh!" That sounds more like a warning growl to the dog and therefore has instant meaning.

Canine thieves are in their element when little kids are carrying cookies in their hands! Your dog will think he's been exceptionally clever if he causes a child to drop a cookie. Bonanza! The easiest solution is to keep dog and children separated at snack time. You must also be sure that the children understand that they must not tease the dog with food—his or theirs. Your dog does not mean to bite the kids, but when he snatches at a tidbit so near the level of his mouth, it can result in an unintended nip.

QUIET DOWN!

If your dog barks excessively, don't bark back. Yelling at him only encourages him to keep it up. Barking at the garbage truck makes perfect sense to the dog—that man is stealing your garbage! When the garbage truck leaves, that spells success to the dog: he has scared away the garbage man with his bark! Pick a command word, something like "Quiet" or "No Bark," to stop his barking. The second he stops, tell him "Good dog" and toss him a toy.

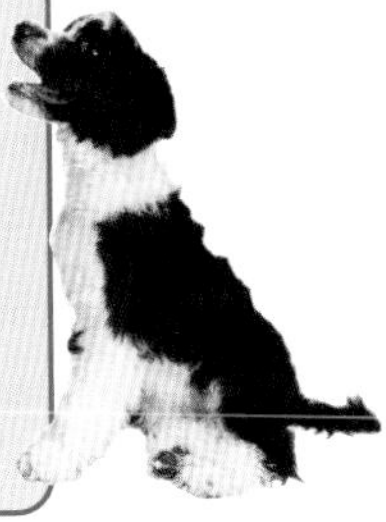

INDEX

Page numbers in ***boldface*** *indicate illustrations.*

My Portuguese Water Dog

PUT YOUR PUPPY'S FIRST PICTURE HERE

Dog's Name ______________________________

Date ____________ Photographer ____________________